THE WINDS OF DESTINY

Second Edition

By

Willie Tee

ISBN: 0-9718784-0-4

This book is printed on acid free paper.

Published by: R&B Trading Company
P.O. Box 5171
Midlothian, Virginia 23112
Telephone: 804-739-8073
Email: Dwindsofdestiny@aol.com

R&B Trading Co – rev.2/20/02

AUTHOR'S FOREWORD

I revised this book on February 12, 2002 to some small degree. The revision does not take anything away from the previous edition of this book, which readers boast is a best seller. Life is all about expressing your opinions, but I deferred from doing that in this book and documented incidents in the way that they occurred. Again, my documentation of certain events is based on my recollections. In some small part, this book is also based on the recollections of my other family members.

I am highly pleased with this Second Edition and the previous edition of this book. The Midwest Book Review's comments and importantly the comments of the readers have sustained me during the promotion of this book. The readers commented that most of the people, who are documented in key roles in this book, are survivors and worthy of the highest praise. Readers adored Uncle Leon and Granny, who are two of the book's characters, the most.

I live in a real world, which I constantly analyze, therefore my own personal beliefs are flexible and subject to change. I would never challenge the beliefs or opinions of anyone else unless there was concrete evidence to do so. Since everything in our world is not concrete, there are things that can never be challenged. Beliefs in the supernatural are some people's own personal beliefs. Therefore, who can safely argue that the supernatural does not exist or that there are powerful forces that we can not see?

I only ask that you remain strong in your beliefs, whatever they maybe, but recognize that there are other influences or things that might be contrary to your beliefs. Then you are being true to yourself and to others. Because, who knows, one day there might be a knock on your door, and out there, a contradiction to certain things that you might have believed in. Therefore, stay flexible and enjoy yourself while reading this book.

THE WINDS OF DESTINY

Originally Titled: *The Death of a Trucker*
1st Copyright (The Essay, *The Death of a Trucker*) issued 12
October 1999, 2nd Copyright (The Novel, *The Death of a Trucker*)
issued January 22, 2001, United States Copyright Office,
Library of Congress, Washington, D.C.
(Non Fiction)

Authored by: Willie Tee

Critical Praise For
Willie Tee And
The Winds of Destiny

The Midwest Book Review of Oregon, Wisconsin wrote, "Set in the 1950s, Willie Tee's The Winds of Destiny is a story about true-life events in the past of author Willie Tee, beginning with the death of his youngest uncle and the dark cloud of a haunting secret that menaced his family. Rural farm life, personal tragedy, and the pervasive belief in voodoo and witchcraft among African Americans in the rural south come to life within the pages of The Winds of Destiny. A charged, thought provoking, deftly written story."

Address To The Spring Creek Baptist Church Congregation: Remarks by Pastor, Dr. Micah McCleary, Author/Co Author of several psychology periodicals and books: "I read The Winds of Destiny. It is good. No, it is better than good."

Reviewed by Mary Wilson (Author of Colorless Soul) 1/29/ 2002: "Mr. Willie Tee, I have not finished reading your book as of yet, but I wanted to reiterate what I wrote to you earlier. You certainly know how to weave a story. I was literally there inside your book through every phase of the story. I visually saw your uncle's truck go over the hillside and I cried as I imagined his fate and that of the driver of the truck. I sat at the funeral and grieved right along with you and your family, and I feel that I have truly met your family. Granny was absolutely delightful and I admired her strength and wisdom. As soon as I finish reading "The Winds of Destiny," I will give you further feedback. I am sure I will not be disappointed at the ending. Thank you so much for writing this book and sharing it with the public."

Reviewed by Victoria Murray (author) 10/22/2001: "An entertaining read! Super job by this talented author.." Victoria Taylor Murray 'Thief Of Hearts' 'Forbidden'

Reviewed by TOM (visitor) 9/21/2001:"EXCELLENT BOOK, ONE OF THE BEST I HAVE READ"

A reviewer, a lover of suspense novels, 23 July 2001 A Real Page-Turner! This novel is a real page-turner. Suspenseful. Keeps the reader's imagination whirling. Everyone can relate to long kept family secrets that if revealed could bring down the strongest of families. Can't wait for the sequel.

Acknowledgements

I dedicate the poem on the next page to my Uncle Leon. I created it during 1975 while stationed in West Germany as a lonely soldier. Sometimes loneliness and isolation help open the mind and things can be seen more clearly.

I told my Uncle Leon some years ago that I was writing a book. He looked at me, paused for a short while and then commented, "Willie, you will have to make the book interesting." This book is about Uncle Leon, and I believe that you will find him a very interesting character.

Uncle Leon was a very charismatic person. He lived longer than some people and a shorter time than some other people have. Of course, long or short lives can be boring lives. Uncle Leon enjoyed life and he would encourage you to enjoy life also and do those things that you desire. We will not live an eternity as the physical beings that we are, so make the best of your life.

I would like to acknowledge my Grandmother or Miss Helen as my father affectionately called her. Without her having given birth to Uncle Leon, this story would not have been possible.

Importantly, I greatly appreciate the love and support that my wife, Ruth, gave me while I wrote this book. I also wish the best of success to the five generations of my family that are now living.

I extend my thanks to Aunt Della, Aunt Virginia, and Aunt Linda for pieces of information that they provided me, while I was writing this book. The information was accurate and invaluable to the writing of this book.

I would also like to acknowledge Mack, who is a life long friend of my uncle, and drove from Georgia to Virginia to honor Uncle Leon at his funeral. We consider Mack as an honorary member of our family, and it is rumored that he might even have closer ties to our family.

I must give all praise to God, the Holy Spirit, who spared me, gave me insight, and guided my hand during the creation of this book. It was God's will that caused this book to be written, and I remain forever his humble servant.

Finally, I would like to honor the memories of my relatives, who have entered into eternity. Their concern and compassion for their other family members will never be forgotten. May they rest in peace.

Nightly Travel

Beacons of light in a stormy night,
Rain splattering rapidly upon a gleaming glass shield,
With a monotonous rhythm,
Roads winding and turning for miles and miles

Their surfaces reflecting glass,
Slippery as water on a wet glass pane.
The sky's eerie glow,
A dog's lonely howl,
Unseen Stars twinkling in the sky.

You have reached solitude,
Your mind wanders,
You think about your first love affair,
About people long forgotten and gone.

Your eyes flicker open and close,
Seeing things that don't exist,
So Wet,
So Wet….
Gone but not forgotten.

TABLE OF CONTENTS

PROLOGUE

Evaluating Superstitions and Other Beliefs

I felt that before you read this book that I should elaborate on some of the superstitions or beliefs that are relative to segments of this story. I think that you will then have a better understanding of certain terminology that is used to portray this story.

My grandparents owned a farm in one of the counties near Wilmington, North Carolina, which is a historic seaport city that played a major role in all wars since The American Revolution. This is the farm where the trucker or my Uncle Leon was reared and the events that occurred there were relative to the trucker's life and destiny.

Wilmington is located near the Outer Banks of North Carolina. The Outer Banks are a chain of barrier islands that sit off the East Coast of the United States. They are minor navigational obstacles to sea faring craft. Many ghostly tales originated in and around Wilmington because of death and destruction precipitated by the Revolutionary and Civil Wars and the many seafaring crafts that visited the city.

Black Beard, the Pirate Captain, conducted his pirating operations at the Outer Banks. Black Beard's hideout was at Ocracoke, Island, a barrier island on the Outer Banks of North Carolina and near Wilmington. Black Beard was killed in a battle with the British Navy at the Outer Banks of North Carolina. It is said that he was a fierce fighter and fought on despite two dozen wounds to his person. The story goes that he was beheaded and his headless body was thrown overboard. It is rumored that though headless, his body swam several times around the ship. So the story goes.

Historic battles were fought at or near Wilmington during the Revolutionary War and the Civil War. The city was a flourishing seaport and vital to providing supplies and munitions to combating armies. Thus, there are many soldiers from those wars buried in and around Wilmington. The city was also the headquarters for the British General, Cornwallis who led the British forces during the Revolutionary War. Perhaps ghostly apparitions of these soldiers can still be seen fighting in eerie battles.

Besides the ghostly tales that have flourished about the soldiers and civilians who died during the Revolutionary and Civil Wars, there are ghostly stories involving the inhabitants of large mansions that are over one hundred years old and located at Wilmington. Even today, it is said that a ghostly apparition of a woman in flowing gowns can be seen during the day or night in one of the old one hundred and fifty year old mansions at Wilmington.

There is also a harrowing story about a train conductor who was working on the railroad tracks in a small town on the outskirts of Wilmington. It seems that while switching some tracks to prevent a deadly collision of two trains, the conductor was decapitated. Legend has it that his head could never be found for burial. According to legend and even modern day research, a light can be seen down a railway track at night. It moves erratically. It is said that it is the ghost of the conductor and he is using a lantern to look for his lost head.

There are also other stories about the ghosts of North Carolina. I recalled seeing a book titled, "The Ghosts of North Carolina."

Being that such beliefs of the supernatural exist, it is easy for people of various cultures to believe that humans can conspire with supernatural forces to bring about a person's early demise or cause a person a wealth of other misfortunes. Supposedly, placing wicked spells on their victims does this. In this story the term "roots" or voodoo is used. Undoubtedly, some of my relatives acquired their beliefs of "roots" from their ancestors, who were brought to this country from West Africa, as slaves several hundred years ago.

Roots are a powerful suggestion, because it is contrived as something that a person can see. Being that it is a visual suggestion, people of questionable character will place an object or talisman at a place where their intended victims can see them. The talisman is designed to look odd and captures one's attention. The talisman can be a pile of whitish powder with blood, chicken feathers or other oddities. One would ask upon seeing the talisman, "What is this? Where did it come from? Who placed it there? What does it mean?" The effectiveness of "roots' is conditional on the beliefs of the person who sees the talisman. The person seeing the talisman realizes that it was placed there for some evil purpose and that harm is intended. Even now during modern times, there are people in mental care facilities, especially in the south, who will adamantly state that voodoo or roots caused their mental or physical problems.

The use of roots is similar to psychological warfare that is used by modern armies. It is used to attack the mind with demoralizing thoughts and feelings. The use of roots reduces a person's morale and feelings of well being.

Fear, jealousies, revenge and hatred are some motivations for people to place visual talismans at the doorsteps or paths of residences or even inside of residences. The placement of talisman is a deplorable act. It can terrify its recipient if the person believes in the suggestion of it. The person placing the talisman could be mentally unstable or have some other insecurity. Realistically, people with such motivations should seek psychiatric help.

During my studies of psychology and other subjects in pursuit of my bachelor's degree in criminal justice, I learned that beliefs in the black arts or witchcraft have been the motive for people committing crimes. Investigators take special training courses to learn more about the beliefs of the blacks arts or witchcraft, so that they can conduct effective investigations. The investigators learn how to evaluate situations where people commit crimes because of beliefs of the black arts or witchcraft.

People who dabble with the supernatural imagine that they have power over their intended victims. Imagining that if they can harm someone with something that leaves no trace, that their identities will remain a secret. However, the practitioners of the black arts arrange their transactions in such a way that their patrons must return for more talismans. The practitioners charge their patrons outlandish amounts of money for each talisman. In essence, a person is paying for something that is impossibility, therefore the transaction is fraudulent. In my opinion, practitioners of the black arts are co-conspirators of deplorable acts. Unfortunately, sometimes the practitioners become the victims of their own fraudulent schemes. In some instances, practitioners of the black arts have been killed by disgruntled patrons. Perhaps, the intended victim or victims were seen even healthier after the purchase and placement of the talisman.

I recall back during the nineteen eighties, I had someone visit me when I resided at North Carolina. He suddenly had a burning desire to visit me. He only visited me one time and never visited again. The visitor stayed at my residence for two days. He was a pleasant houseguest but I was suspicious of his visit, because he had declined many of my previous invitations. Upon his departure, he stated that he had left his shoes in my house. The visitor ran into my house and then came out empty handed. He then stated that he was mistaken because his shoes were packed with his other clothing. A short time after his departure, I discovered a talisman on the foot of my bed. My visitor traveled one hundred miles to deliver a visual suggestion. Later, he boldly made strange comments to suggest that he had placed the talisman there. He provided no sound justifications for his actions. The visitor did tell me vehemently some time later that my days were numbered. Though, he was much older than I was, he stated that I would not outlive him.

I am here to report that he died three years ago and I am still flourishing. He did call several times after the placing of the talisman to inquire about my health. I wonder if the practitioner he consulted with had a refund policy? I stated the aforementioned to make a point.

When I was stationed in South Korea and bivouacked near a graveyard, some Korean soldiers under my supervision were antsy. Upon me inquiring, they pointed out that we were camped at a cemetery. The soldiers were concerned and it supports that superstitions exist worldwide. I consoled the Korean soldiers by stating that we would only have to worry about the living harming us that night as the dead are harmless. They laughed nervously and our night's sleep there was uneventful.

Scientists say that there are about eight dimensions here on earth, including the one that we exist in. Early religious scholars during the Renaissance Period in Europe during the fourteenth through seventeenth centuries speculated that people are carbon copies of their spiritual selves. The scholars meant that we are spiritual beings who are represented by earthly humans. The scholars implied that when our human bodies cease to exist, our spiritual essences would continue to exist.

During my studies of the History of Christianity, I learned that man, throughout time, believed there are both the forces of good and evil in our universe. I was taught that the coming of Christ was essential to insure that we realize those forces. Therefore, when our spiritual selves leave our earthly bodies, we must go towards the light. However, you must believe in the creator of the heavens and the earth to go towards the light.

Since it is believed that there are forces of evil a foot, it would be foolish to dabble with the black arts. Like a song says, "Put your hand in the hand of the man who stilled the waters." With all that said, I hope you enjoy reading my book. Believe it or not, this story is based on true events.

Chapter One

The Days of Sorrow

(1957-1997)

I stood at the foot of his grave, misty-eyed for the first time, though I had visited his grave several times before. My sorrow of his death was made even harsher by a newly installed grave marker at the head of my uncle's grave. I noticed that the grave marker was a large bronze plate laid on top of a salt and pepper colored granite slab. The grave marker and its base were laid flat on the ground and surrounded by lush green grass. The bronze plate was inscribed with "Uncle Leon's name, 1946-1997, PVT, US Army." With my head bowed solemnly, I reminisced on the events leading up to my uncle's death, and the traumatic effects it had on his family afterwards.

Like a bad dream, my Great Aunt Gracie , who was my grandmother's sister, died when she was almost one hundred-years-old, and about nine months prior to Uncle Leon. A few months after my great aunt's death, Uncle Leon's sister, Aunt Eloise, died from a kidney-related illness. Then along came the death of Uncle Leon during January 1997, about five months after the death of Aunt Eloise. I knew my great aunt's death was imminent due to her incredible life span. Aunt Eloise was not in the best of health prior to her death, but her death was still a shock, because it came so unexpectedly.

I recalled my college psychology courses, which outlined how people react to the death of loved ones. First there is shock or disbelief, which is followed by depression. Then there are feelings of guilt with thoughts that perhaps something could have been done to prevent the death. Then, there is a period of grieving. Fi-

1

nally, there is coping with the death, followed by a period of healing and coming to terms with the mourner's own mortality.

I remember sitting down suddenly, as if I had been struck on the chest with a baseball bat, when I received word of Uncle Leon's death. A man, who I often thought of as indestructible or practically immortal, was gone or dead. I remember him driving his big rig (tractor and trailer) over ice and snow and up and down treacherous mountains during the worst weather conditions known to man.

I reflect back to the time when Uncle Leon, who is nine years my senior, built a go-cart and placed a farming gas turbine engine on it. I recalled commenting to my uncle, "Small car with a big motor." In my adolescent mind, the go-cart and the turbine engine were not compatible. You will never see it in any record book, but Uncle Leon's go-cart surpassed all land speed records for go-carts that day. A person might now surmise that this was the go-carts maiden and final voyage. Reminiscent of the sinking of the Titanic, the go-cart ended up submerged in the bottom of a deep irrigation ditch, a heap of twisted and bent metal. I saw my uncle, who lied torn and tattered in a cornfield. This was not to be the last of uncle's death defying stunts as a teenager.

I remember my uncle now as being gregarious and light hearted. Uncle Leon had a knack of remembering life threatening incidents around the farm where people barely escaped by the skin of their teeth. He would comically recall the incidents and accompany them with physical theatrics. There seemed to be no limits to Uncle Leon's strange but funny sense of humor.

I remember Uncle Leon introducing me to the art of fisticuffs or boxing when I was almost five years old. He was nine years older than I. Uncle Leon taught me how to take up a good fighting stance with legs and feet planted firmly on the ground. During my boxing classes, which were administered by Uncle Leon, he encouraged me to throw hard punches into his outstretched hands. My small tight fists would emit loud slapping sounds as I hammered my uncle's hands. He then encouraged me to hit his hands even harder. I hammered his hands even harder and Uncle Leon laughed heartily and told me that he had enough. The things that Uncle Leon trained and skilled me in were confidence builders, but he also taught me self-control and how to be a sportsman.

At age five I was stout and muscular, and devoured whole plates of food that my smiling granny served me. I helped my Uncle John, who is Uncle Leon's older brother, with his carpentry work. On occasions nails would bend as he drove them into a wood structure he was building or repairing. Uncle John would pause with his skilled hammering, while I grasped the bent nails with my hands and ripped them out of the wood.

After I got over the initial shock of that dreadful phone call about Uncle Leon's death, I immediately turned in my police officer gear and went directly to Uncle Leon's house. When I arrived, I comforted Aunt Shirley who already had a house full of other relatives. On the verge of tears and wringing her hands, Aunt Shirley outlined the grim details of the trucking accident in Tennessee. According to Aunt Shirley, Uncle Leon's big rig had slid off a mountain in Tennessee. Uncle Leon and his trainee were killed instantly. Aunt Shirley then remarked that Uncle Leon had telephoned her several days before the accident and complained that snowy and icy road conditions were causing delays during his trips. Aunt Shirley then pointed out that the trucking firm told her that the trainee was driving when the accident occurred. I raised my eyebrows and was puzzled as to why Uncle Leon would let the trainee drive in the mountains during the icy winter. I did not make any comments about the trainee being allowed to drive during hazardous road conditions in the mountains. It seemed that my Uncle as the more experienced driver should have been driving the truck. Aunt Shirley had received only sketchy details about the accident. I then remarked that I had driven through the mountains of Tennessee myself. I recalled renting a motel room in the same town where Uncle Leon's fatal accident occurred. This only added to the irony of the situation.

I then shuddered in recollection of the high mountains of Tennessee and the mountains' treacherous up and down slopes and breath taking curves. Without thinking, I remarked that from the peaks of the mountains, the houses in the valleys below were the size of toothpicks. I commented that the plunge from the mountains to the valleys below would be devastating. I saw Aunt Shirley's eyes widen and it seemed that she trembled. I changed the subject but then thought to myself that there would be nothing recognizable of a truck or human after a plunge like that. I was concerned that I would never see Uncle Leon's again and his funeral would be a closed coffin affair. I then felt that it would be even more difficult for me to obtain closure concerning his death. I needed to see Uncle Leon and come to grips with the fact that Uncle Leon was gone.

I was at Aunt Shirley's house for almost thirty minutes when my youngest aunt, Aunt Linda, arrived with her husband, Stephanie. Aunt Linda, an attractive lady, looked very solemn and grief stricken. She sat down on a chair near me with her head bowed and turned slightly to the side. Her husband, Stephanie sat near her, upright and rigid and puffed slowly on a smoking pipe, which was emitting a pleasant aroma of smoking tobacco.

Aunt Shirley approached us and sat down. She commented that she needed information from Aunt Linda and I to create an obituary for Uncle Leon. Aunt Shirley was struggling to maintain her composure during what had to be one of the worst days of her life. Aunt Linda wrote down names of blood relatives whose names we felt should appear on the obituary and calculated the total number of nieces and nephews that Uncle Leon had. When Aunt Linda and I had completed the lists of relatives for the obituary, Aunt Shirley asked if his older brother, John, would be attending the funeral services. Aunt Linda commented that she did not really know if he would attend, and I noticed that her face was devoid of any emotions when she spoke.

I looked upon Aunt Shirley's countenance and it seemed that she was unable to digest Aunt Linda's comments. I quickly interjected that Uncle John was wheel chair bound and really not able to travel great distances from home. I felt that my remarks would clear up any thoughts or speculations that Aunt Shirley might have, when Aunt Linda commented again that it was hard to say if he would attend. She stated, "I just don't know." I decided to let the issue rest as I was getting signals from Aunt Linda's body language that she did not desire to discuss Uncle John's impending presence at the funeral.

I silently reflected over Aunt Linda's comments to Aunt Shirley's inquiries about Uncle John. My family has resided in the rural counties of North Carolina since the Emancipation Proclamation. I know of our tendency to be secretive with our thoughts and feelings. I recalled growing up during the late 1950s (1957-1961) on the small family farm in a county of North Carolina. It was during a time of segregation between blacks and whites and both races had separate schools, water fountains and meeting places. It was a time of suspicion and a lack of trust. President Dwight Eisenhower was in office and Premier Nikita Khrushchev was the President of Russia. Things were very tense between the United States and Russia, as these were the early years of the Cold War. When I was four years old, my younger aunts and uncle often spoke of the Russians invading us. I did not think of Russians as being human and in my childish mind envisioned them as a huge swarm of bloodthirsty locusts that would decimate our home. I had no concept of how big the United States was and where the Russians actually lived.

My world was within the close confines of the family farm and the majority of my grandparents' children either resided with them or on adjacent properties near my grandparent's house. My aunts and uncles could converse with each other by yelling up the dirt road that was dusty during the summers and muddy during the winter. The country road was lined on both sides by trees and pockmarked with numerous potholes. There was a ditch on one side of the dirt road, which had a small clear stream running through it. I spent time during the summer and winter playing in the stream with my toy boats. Those times as a child were so adventurous and carefree.

My mother (Annie), my siblings (Helen and George), and I lived a stone's throw up the road from Granny's house in a clapboard two room house that Uncle John built for my mother. My Mother gave Uncle John, her brother, $200.00 for building the small house, but the house was presentable and kept out the rain, cold and wind. The small house or shanty was not insulated and I could lie in bed and peep through the cracks of the wooden siding of our house. I could see the woods behind our house and trails or footpaths that snaked through the woods.

During the winter months, our two room house was heated by a pot belly wood stove constructed of galvanized steel and tin. I would jump out of bed on those chilly mornings and stand close to the stove. The sides of the stove would be a bright cherry red, and very hot. One unfortunate morning, I stood too close to the wood stove and emitted a surprised yelp. I jumped back quickly from the stove as it seared the skin on my left upper thigh. Needless to say, this was the first and last time that I was burned by the pot-belly stove. I learned that hot stoves were a source of warmth and comfort if I stood at a distance from them.

Our small shanty house did not have indoor plumbing and we were forced to deal with personal urges by visiting an outhouse situated at the rear of the shanty. The roof of our shanty was constructed with sheets of tin. On days and nights when it would rain, I could hear the rhythmic splattering sounds of raindrops on our tin roof. The sounds of the rain striking the roof of our house had a consistent pattern. After listening to it for a while, my eyes would become droopy, and I would fall into a deep and pleasant sleep. I often reminisce now back to those times and wonder why anyone would want to grow up and leave behind one of the best times of their life, their childhood, as mere memories.

About forty feet from our shanty was another larger shanty where my Aunt Peggy lived with her only son, Howard. My Aunt Margaret and her two sons, William and Earl lived in Aunt Peggy's shanty also. Aunt Peggy and Aunt Margaret were the older sisters of Uncle Leon. Like my mother, they had married and had children. My two aunts separated from their husbands after marriage and returned to my grandparents' farm. Aunt Peggy had purchased nine acres of timberland near my grandparent's farm. She had the portion of the timberland near the dirt road cleared off and on this she built her shanty. Both Aunt Peggy and Aunt Margaret married soldiers who served during the Korean War Era.

I would often listen to hushed conversations among my grandmother and her older daughters about wicked spells that people could cast on each other. North Carolina and South Carolina were hot beds of discussions about voodoo or what most blacks referred to as "roots". This is not relative to genealogical roots but the black magic roots.

We were country folk and stories or tales of the supernatural seemed to go hand in hand with our isolation from nearby cities and the dark and forbidding woods that surrounded our houses and farm. At night the wind would howl and whisper as it blew blasts of air through the woods near our house. The trees would creak and sway and cast eerie shadows on the walls of our shanty. I would huddle and shiver beneath the quilts, with them pulled over my head to ward off the goblin like shadows that danced on the walls of the shanty.

As a toddler, I had rather large ears for hushed conversations. On occasions I crept too close to the older women, who would playfully scowl at me and say, "Boy, you get away from here." "It ain't polite to listen to older folk's conversations." I would leave the presence of the older women and strain my ears to soak up their conversations. I learned that "roots" could be sulfur powder, blood and perhaps chicken feathers or other talismans strewn across a path that a person would take to reach their home. According to the older women, the presence of such items would cause people much concern and then they would gather up a few hundred dollars and travel to South Carolina. I learned that these trips to South Carolina were for the purpose of consulting with "Root Doctors" and it was rumored that the best practitioners of the art resided at South Carolina. According to some stories I heard, a person who had roots or a wicked spell placed on them, could have it reversed at a price. It seemed that there were some powerful Root Doctors that could determine who placed evil spells on an undeserving person and sold talismans or roots to the victims to cast wicked counter spells on their tormenters. My eyes would widen, the hairs on my neck would rise, and I would shiver as they recounted their spine tingling stories.

Aunt Virginia told me later during my adult life, after I confessed to her about my eavesdropping, that I was fortunate. She explained that during her early childhood in the early nineteen fifties, the punishment for eavesdropping was a spray of tobacco spit in the face from an adult. I had seen some of my relatives spit out snuff and tobacco juice before, and they were very accurate at hitting spittoons and other targets at substantial distances.

Suspicions about roots or other supernatural events were sometimes blamed for people's untimely deaths, thus the web of suspicion became even more intricate. The web of suspicion limited social contacts with people who were not direct family members and in some families it restricted certain family secrets to the older family members. Over the years, keeping family secrets became a structured way of life for most family members. They would not

8

discuss certain family issues with outsiders. They would even deny the existence of past family problems.

I did not know during my early childhood of the secret that haunted our family farm. The secret had brought sorrow to the lives of my relatives who lived at the farm. It would also place a burden on me during my later childhood and adult life. Years later, as a teenager, I would learn of the awful secret. I would later question the wisdom of keeping such a secret, after its magnitude had sent shock waves of repercussions throughout the family. It was unimaginable that such a thing had happened on this picturesque farm, which was always filled with laughter and cheer during my childhood.

My thoughts were suddenly refocused on the situation at hand when Aunt Linda nudged me with her elbow and made some comments about Uncle Leon's obituary that we were crafting. Aunt Linda and I completed the draft of the obituary, and I told Aunt Shirley that I would be back the next day to assist her with some other matters. I then departed for my drive home.

I did not pay much attention to the fourteen-mile drive because I was still stunned from having received word of Uncle Leon's death. I was driving my black Chevrolet Silverado Pickup Truck, but had neglected to turn on the radio. Many thoughts swirled through my mind about things that needed to be done for Uncle Leon's funeral.

According to Aunt Shirley, Uncle Leon's remains were still at Pulaski, Tennessee and a funeral home several miles from Aunt Shirley's residence had been selected to perform funeral services. Since Uncle Leon had died today or on a Friday, little could be done over the weekend to transport his remains back to his city of residence. Aunt Shirley told me that she and her daughters had selected Wednesday as the day of the funeral. Needless to say, I was concerned about the time situation, because it would be Monday until we could sit down with the funeral home director and make some solid arrangements.

Without a doubt, my truck drove itself home because I was barely conscious of even driving it. One might compare my truck to a faithful horse that will always bring you home even though you might be sleeping while astride it.

I drove up into the driveway of my gray two-story colonial home with its rust colored shutters. My wife, Ruth often commented that the rust colored shutters and our rambling colonial house reminded her of a barn. I parked my truck in the driveway and walked inside the house through the side door. My wife, Ruth, looked at me with compassion and concern. I returned her gaze and shook my head slowly. Ruth then told me that she had telephoned my Aunt Virginia, who is Uncle Leon's sister, and slightly older than him. Ruth commented that Aunt Virginia was saddened by the bad news.

I then telephoned Aunt Virginia myself and she told me that Granny was managing well under the circumstances. I informed Aunt Virginia that Uncle Leon's remains were at a funeral home at Pulaski Tennessee, though Aunt Shirley did not request any funeral home to remove his remains from the hospital. I told her that there would be delays, because of the weekend and funeral homes being closed, in the transportation of his remains back to his city of residence. I also told her that the funeral was tentatively scheduled for Wednesday. I asked her to notify our relatives of the tentative funeral arrangements. Aunt Virginia then made comments concerning Uncle Leon team driving with another driver and the risks involved. I assured her that Uncle Leon and I had a conversation about this issue prior to his death, and that he decided to team drive despite the risks.

Chapter Two

According to Tradition

(1994-1997)

The next day, Saturday, I arrived at Aunt Shirley's house after noontime and brought a large bucket of Kentucky Fried Chicken with me. Bringing food to the home of the deceased is a traditional thing in most southern states. It might be traditional through out the country, but I have lived only in the south all of my life. I could not imagine Aunt Shirley and her daughters cooking during their time of sorrow. I surmised that many people, friends and relatives would be coming over to Uncle Leon's house to sit for long periods of time to comfort his family. It was traditional for the visiting mourners to eat some of the food that they and other mourners brought to the home of the deceased. It seemed practical because some mourners would drive great distances to visit and the offering of food by the deceased's family helped defray expenses.

Well, Uncle Leon would have his own opinion about the gathering of mourners. Uncle Leon lived a simple life and did not like a lot of extravagances. He seemed to desire only the basic necessities of life for himself but the best of things for his wife and family. I mirror my uncle's outlook on life, because in my opinion material things are of no great importance. I figure that a man can only wear or use a small portion of what he possesses in life. The remainder of what he possesses, or the greater portion, is acquired to impress others.

Personally, I feel that academic achievements and the nurturing and education of one's children are greater rewards than wealth.

Conscience: *"Willie, you left something out. Aunt Shirley told you about a phone call that she got from Uncle Leon's family in North Carolina."* I responded, *"Well, do we need to put that in this* *story?" The voice responded, " Well, its important that you as an author capture the significance of what your are portraying.*

While I was at Aunt Shirley's house, she mentioned that my relatives asked if she would permit Uncle Leon to be buried in the family cemetery at North Carolina. Aunt Shirley then paused to get my reaction. I commented that it would be a long drive for her to visit his grave at North Carolina, unless she never intended to visit him often. I then expounded that since Uncle Leon spent most of his life intimately with her, that it should be her decision. Aunt Shirley then responded that she would have him buried in Virginia near her and his children.

I then reminisced about being at Cousin Earl's funeral wake about two years earlier. Cousin Earl was about forty-one years old when he died from an apparent aneurysm. The wake is customarily held the day before the funeral and usually at the Funeral Home's Chapel. Relatives and friends are given the opportunity to gather and view the deceased's remains as the person lies in a state of slumber in the coffin. I guess the wake helps relatives confront the deceased relative's demise. It supports confirmation, because people often say after hearing of a loved one's death, that they just don't believe that the person is dead. They are in a state of disbelief. However, when they attend the wake and view the deceased's remains the reality of it all sinks in.

I remember reading something in my sociology book about a person's expected behavior during a variety of life's event. In my family, a visual show of emotion with screaming and crying is acceptable at a wake and funeral. However, a display of sadness with composure is also acceptable.

Uncle Leon asked me about the identity of numerous persons who paraded by Cousin Earl's coffin and viewed his remains. There was no problem with Uncle Leon asking who the mourners were, but honestly, I did not know sixty percent of the people there by name. Most of them, I had never seen before during my lifetime.

This is always the situation at a wake of funeral. There was a problem however with Uncle Leon asking about the mourner's identities, because he was asking questions about them in a loud tone of voice. I saw the mourners cock their heads in Uncle Leon's direction, whenever he would ask who the persons were. I whispered to Uncle Leon in a soft voice that I did not know some of the mourners. I also wished that Uncle Leon would stop asking questions about the mourners, because he was the center of attention. Cousin Earl's brother, Cousin William, was sitting in front of us. Cousin William then turned around and glared at Uncle Leon and me. He asked us to walk outside with him. I thought to myself, oh well, here comes controversy. I was a police officer back then, and I dealt with too much controversy on the job. Cousin William told Uncle Leon and I that he was appalled at our loud behavior. I gave a short apology and the serious expression on Cousin Williams' face changed to that of a broad smile. Uncle Leon justified his behavior by quoting a scripture from the bible about rejoicing people's deaths because of the promise of eternal life. I guess this was his way of apologizing, but the expression on Cousin William's face earlier was enough to provide us both with an immediate promise of eternal life.

I was relieved that things were resolved easily, because our family always had controversies at family funerals. Without fail, someone would make an inappropriate comment and tempers would flare. There were times when Granny, who was well over ninety years old, would come flying downstairs or upstairs with the ease of a hurdle jumper to intervene in disagreements at family funerals. She would raise her walking cane in a threatening way at the offenders and her eyes would flash. Granny did not get upset often but when she did, she would deliver a sound scolding. The scolding would be replete with remarks about the offenders' past misdeeds and their need to do some praying to redeem themselves. Granny had a flare for using words like "strumpet", "old

13

dogs", "devilish hounds" and "trifling". Never have I heard Granny curse. Granny has always been God fearing and a frequent attendee at church.

I met with Aunt Shirley on the second day after Uncle Leon's death, which was on a Sunday. I then found out that Uncle Leon's death was wrought with complications. Aunt Shirley reiterated as she had done earlier, that someone had authorized Uncle Leon's remains to be picked up at the hospital morgue and transported to a local funeral home at Pulaski, Tennessee. Aunt Shirley was at a loss as to whom authorized the moving of his remains, because a funeral home in the city where Aunt Shirley resided had been contracted to do the funeral services. I saw the look of consternation on Aunt Shirley's face because she had set Uncle Leon's funeral tentatively for Wednesday. The transportation of his remains on Monday from Tennessee appeared too close to the day of the funeral. I knew that my relatives would be arriving Tuesday for the funeral. I then thought about Murphy's law and things that could potentially go wrong on Monday. My thoughts were disheartening, because I knew that the family would want to have a traditional wake for Uncle Leon on Tuesday, the day prior to his funeral. I also took into consideration that Aunt Shirley would not meet officially with the undertaker until Monday to make detailed funeral arrangements.

I have not described the personalities of the blood kin of Uncle Leon as of yet. We are fairly easy to get along with if things are running smoothly. With my relatives grieving over the death of Uncle Leon, who rated very highly in the beloved category, problems with the funeral would irritate them. Surely, some of my relatives would be agitated if the funeral were wrought with problems. Since I was one of the few relatives who lived near Uncle Leon, I would also be blamed to some degree for any problems. However, to preclude any finger pointing, I decided to assist Uncle Leon's immediate family and ensure that certain aspects of the impending funeral were prepared appropriately.

I went to work on the evening shift after departing Aunt Shirley's house. I was patrolling the hallways of the Veterans Affairs Hospital, when one of the hospital's janitorial workers approached me. He approached me and stated, "You must be Willie and the nephew of the trucker who got killed." The janitor then explained that a relative of his is a trucker and knew my Uncle Leon. The relative of the janitor had told him about Uncle Leon's tragic accident and the fact that Uncle Leon often spoke of having a nephew who worked as a police officer at the Veterans Affairs Hospital. The janitor then elaborated that though his relative did not work at the same trucking firm as Uncle Leon, his relative, a trucker had met Uncle Leon. Then oddly, the janitor said, "Your uncle told my relative that he was going to stop driving trucks at the end of this February." The janitor then gave his condolences. I then pondered on the janitor's comments and thought how strange it was that his tragic accident occurred before he stopped driving.

On Monday, late in the evening, and two days before his funeral, Uncle Leon's remains arrived at Virginia by airplane from Tennessee. His remains were picked up by the local funeral home at the airport and taken to their mortuary. I was at the funeral home late that evening with Cousin Nicole, who is Uncle Leon's daughter. I got into a mild argument with a funeral home attendant about the whereabouts of Uncle Leon. I was promised earlier that he would arrive at about four in the evening, but it was now eight o'clock in the evening and he had not arrived. I instructed the attendant to contact Aunt Shirley upon the arrival of my uncle's remains. The attendant got curt about who was paying for the funeral. I assured him that I was acting on behalf of Aunt Shirley. I then advised him to do as I had instructed. At this point the attendant had two strikes against him. I then reflected that not all people possess common sense and good judgement.

I arrived at Aunt Shirley's house minutes later. She then informed me that she had received a phone call from the mortuary that Uncle Leon's remains had arrived there. I then relaxed and felt that I could rest easier

In retrospect, I recall visiting my uncle unexpectedly six months prior to his death and saw him changing a gas filter on his car. Uncle Leon had his car raised up on a bumper jack, and I spied him underneath the car changing the gas filter. I chided him for not using the proper safety precautions, because the car should have been resting on jack stands. I then saw the car began to sway, and I yelled at my uncle to roll out from under the car. As Uncle Leon rolled out of harm's way, the car fell with a heavy thump onto the pavement. The jack had slipped off the bumper. Uncle Leon then laughed at his close brush with death. I stormed off to get several jack stands from his storage shed.

I often reflect on this particular incident, because I happened to visit Uncle Leon at a critical time to prevent him from having an accident. The car falling onto him would have been either fatal or he would have been severely crippled. The incident was strange because it was very seldom that I would catch Uncle Leon at home. Uncle Leon drove for a trucking firm and it kept him on the road frequently during weekends. I was a Police Officer and worked two weekends per month, therefore we met on rare occasions. I know that if I had not gone to his house on that particular week-end, his untimely demise would have not been from the results of a trucking accident. Theoretically, Uncle Leon would have not been available to train the driver who was at the wheel of the big rig during their fatal crash. I can see now that my visit to Uncle Leon's house that Sunday was an event that somehow foreshadowed other future events.

I remember during the winter of 1996, that the State of Virginia received a snowstorm of blizzard proportion, especially in the central part of the state where Uncle Leon and I resided. There was a foot or more of snow on the ground. I was a police officer at a Veterans Affairs Hospital and drove to work during the snowy and treacherous road conditions in my four- wheel drive Chevrolet truck. A day or two after the massive snow storm, I had a day off and received a telephone call from Uncle Leon. Uncle Leon inquired as to whether I had a hacksaw or some other metal cutting instrument. I pondered his request and then remembered having a metal cutting blade on my circular electrical handsaw. I had installed some landscaping timbers on both sides of my driveway, which paralleled the length of the driveway on both sides. I had used the metal cutting blade on my electric circular saw to cut six-foot metal rebars or stakes into one-foot sections. I drove the metal rebars through predrilled holes on the landscaping timbers into the ground beneath the timbers to secure them in place. I informed Uncle Leon that I had something that would suit his needs. We agreed to meet at his home.

Upon my arrival at Uncle Leon's house, I retrieved the circular saw from my truck and greeted Uncle Leon at the front porch of his house. With his luminous eyes, Uncle Leon reminded me of a Koala Bear. Uncle Leon had a long length of a medium size linked chain in his kitchen. He then used my circular saw to cut the chain into three equal lengths, which equated to almost four feet per length. I marveled at my saw's efficiency, because the cutting of the chain took about three minutes. I then looked at Uncle Leon quizzically, because it seemed that he was in a hurry. Uncle Leon observed my confused facial expression and commented that he was going to place the lengths of chain around rear tires of his tractor or big truck that was stuck on a patch of ice. I had noticed Uncle Leon's assigned truck, without its trailer, or "Bobtailed", as truckers would say it, parked in front of his house when I arrived. Uncle Leon explained that the lengths of chain placed around the rear tires would function as improvised snow chains.

I then followed Uncle Leon to his tractor and he used long

bolts with nuts to attach the lengths of chain through the slotted tire rims and over the threaded surface of three tires. I noticed that the rear of the truck had two axles. Two sets of double tires were attached to the front axle and two sets of double tires were attached to the rear axle. Since the two front tires on his tractor were not pulling wheels, there was no need to equip them with lengths of chain. My uncle placed the lengths of chain on the outer wheel of the double wheels on the right and left rear of the truck. I surmised that if my uncle could drive off the large patch of ice under his tractor that he would have no other concerns because the unplowed roadway near his house had deep furrows in the snow where other vehicles had passed. The sun had warmed up things since the snowstorm and some of the snow was turning to slush.

Uncle Leon, who was wearing a billed cap rakishly on his head, stepped onto the running board of his white tractor, which had the name of the trucking company emblazoned on it. He stepped into the cab of the truck. Uncle Leon then turned on the ignition and paused to allow the glow plugs of the engine to warm to a temperature to ignite the sluggish diesel fuel that propelled the huge truck. I heard a loud humming noise as the glow plugs warmed. Then the truck cranked up and started running with a deafening and rhythmic hum. My uncle placed the truck into a forward low range gear and one set of double tires on the left rear axle of the double tandem of axles began to spin on the ice furiously. The chain attached to the set of tires began to spin and clank loudly as showers of ice and slushy snow were thrown up into the air at the truck's rear. Uncle Leon then engaged the front axle simultaneously with the rear spinning tires, and one set of tires on the front axle began to rotate and spew showers of ice and slush. However, the huge truck remained trapped or marooned on the patch of ice. Uncle Leon ceased his efforts, and then geared his truck to turn the huge sets of tires on the opposing sides of the front and rear axles. I noted that the huge tires were spinning in a crisscross fashion, therefore the two sets of tires on the front axle never turned at the same time. This was also the case with both sets of rear wheels. I remembered the Hummers or all terrain vehicles that I drove while in the United States Army Military Police Corps. The wheels and axles of the Hummer were also geared and arranged transmatically to reduce power to a wheel that was spinning and give it to another wheel that had more traction. Similar to a baby crawling on his hands and knees, vehicles geared in this way can inch their way through thick muck and mire. Of course, this multiple wheel gearing system is not always a sure thing, because when none of the wheels have traction, the vehicle is stuck. Vehicles equipped with winches have additional alternatives of freeing themselves, if a tree or other sufficient anchor point is nearby to attach a cable to.

Uncle Leon continued to spin the rear wheels of his truck and the showers of ice and slush turned to showers of asphalt and then dirt. Still the huge truck did not move and remained on the sheet of ice. Suddenly, I saw two lengths of chain fly off two of the rear wheels. Uncle Leon then terminated his attempts to dislodge the truck and jumped from the cab. Uncle Leon then gazed at my full size four-wheel drive truck. He glanced at me and smiled slightly. I slowly shook my head. I surmised that my truck was in no way proportional to his huge tractor. The thought of pulling his tractor off the ice with my truck was not a consideration. Uncle Leon did not seem disheartened, and announced that he had another plan. Uncle Leon then summoned a wrecker that was contracted to assist stranded truckers.

While awaiting the arrival of the wrecker, I discussed with Uncle Leon that the roads were still icy and treacherous in some areas of Virginia. He stated that once he got to the depot to pick up the trailer, that it would put more weight on the rear tires of the tractor. Uncle Leon pointed out that he would gain enough traction that way to make a trip.

Thirty minutes later, a small antiquated wrecker arrived and a blonde hair man wearing hip wader boots, and resembled the British singer, Tom Jones, disembarked from the wrecker. I raised my eyebrows upon seeing the wrecker, because it seemed inadequate for pulling the huge tractor off the ice. The wrecker driver then attached the towing cable on the boom of his wrecker to the rear of the tractor. He angled the rear of the wrecker towards the rear of the tractor. The wrecker driver then engaged the winch of the wrecker and the towing platform and boom of the wrecker began to creak and tilt upwards as the cable pulled the rear of the truck slowly across the ice. I moved away, because it seemed that the cable might snap or the whole towing platform of the wrecker would be ripped completely off. Miraculously, the small wrecker was able to winch the rear of the tractor off the icy patch. Uncle Leon signed the wrecker's driver tow bill and then jumped into the cab of his truck. He looked at me from the cab of his truck and commented, "Well Willie, time for me to roll. See you next time."

Uncle Leon then shifted his truck into low gear and departed his house. The wrecker and I were driving behind Uncle Leon when he made a turn to get onto the major thoroughfare. There were some patches of ice near a stop sign and upon stopping for traffic, Uncle Leon's truck was stuck again on a patch of ice. The wrecker driver then pulled the truck off the ice with the wrecker again and my uncle continued on his trip.

Chapter Three

The Burial of a Trucker

(1997)

On Tuesday, the day before Uncle Leon's funeral services, I visited the mortuary. during the afternoon hours. I wanted to verify the remains as Uncle Leon's because of continuous delays with the shipment of his remains. Uncle Preston, his wife Aunt Della and Cousin Harriet, who is Aunt Della's daughter, had arrived from their homes at North Carolina earlier during the day. They were parked outside of the mortuary in a dark blue Lincoln Continental. My relatives' faces were filled with sorrow and emotions.

Before I entered the preparation room, a woman mortuary assistant warned the hair stylist that I was entering the room. Uncle Preston, who is Uncle Leon's brother-in-law, accompanied me when I walked into the preparation room. I then saw Uncle Leon, who was draped from the neck down with a white sheet and his head was raised up on a block device. Upon seeing him, I concluded that Uncle Leon was in fact gone, because nothing else would have convinced me otherwise. A mortuary assistant was styling his hair.

My curiosity about the announcement of my arrival was explained when the stylist gazed at me and stated that I bore an uncanny resemblance to my uncle. This also explained why the woman who saw me, as I entered the mortuary, reacted to me in a curious way. I figured that if the stylist had seen me walking in unannounced, he would have surmised that it was Uncle Leon at first glance. I surmised that mistaking me for Uncle Leon, the deceased, would have been enough to startle even the bravest of men.

You never know how people are going to react when they are confronted with the death of a loved one. Uncle Preston commented to the hair stylist that he was combing Uncle Leon's hair to the rear, whereas Uncle Leon always wore his hair combed forward. Uncle Preston then touched Uncle Leon's hair and smoothed it forward with his hand. The hair stylist paused and then commented that he could rearrange Uncle Leon's hair to the front. I was at odds as to what to say and was thinking that at this point, that Uncle Leon's hairstyle was of no great importance. It was painfully apparent that after Uncle Leon's funeral, that the styling of his hair would be of no importance. I reasoned that death was a done deal and the dead have no concerns or worries. I asked the stylist if Uncle Leon's wife was satisfied with the hairstyle and he remarked that she had made no specific comments about it. I was trying to handle the situation diplomatically, but I wanted Uncle Preston, who was wrought with grief, to come to certain realizations. At the same time, I also realized that Uncle Preston wanted to insure the integrity of Uncle Leon's usual appearance. I then commented that Uncle Leon always combed his hair forward. I had witnessed him combing his hair that way for years. The hair stylist nodded and Uncle Leon continued his journey into eternity, but now wearing his customary hairstyle.

A mortuary director greeted me as I departed the mortuary with Uncle Preston. He remembered me, because I had accompanied Aunt Shirley the day before to make Uncle Leon's funeral arrangement. I asked him about the military honor guard as Uncle Leon had served in the military. The director commented that the arrangements had been made, but he seemed reluctant to integrate the military honor guard into the arrangements. I was able to determine later that the real issue was about time. My feeling on the issue of time was that the mortuary was paid handsomely for the funeral. Uncle Leon's burial was not going to be a rushed affair. My patience with the funeral director had begun to wear thin.

It always seems that the further you venture south concerning the southern states, the more elaborate the funeral arrangements. This means that no one, to include the mortuary staff is in a hurry to bury the deceased. It is guaranteed that during the church service for the deceased that there will be the appropriate displays of grief. It is not advisable to put a time limit on how long the outbursts of grieving will last during a funeral service. I can say honestly, that anyone trying to impose time limitations would be digging their own grave. I have seen most funeral homes directors and assistants at funerals in the south look more grief stricken than immediate family members have. I praise them for their professionalism and stoic appearance during a family's time of grief. In my family, the dead are afforded the utmost respect and rightfully so.

My sister Helen, her son, Jermaine, and Cousin William arrived from North Carolina late in the evening on Tuesday before Granny and my other relatives. I drove them to the chapel of the mortuary to attend the wake. Aunt Shirley, her three daughters (Angela, Nicole and Bridget) and two grandsons were at the wake. Uncle Leon lied in his coffin with a folded American Flag placed near his shoulder.

I walked up to Uncle Leon's coffin during the wake and was accompanied by my sister, Helen and Cousin William. Uncle Leon was dressed splendidly in a dark blue suit. There were no indications that he had been in a fatal truck crash. Aunt Shirley had told me that Uncle Leon was also going to be dressed in under wear of the finest silk. I do not know if they went to that extravagance. Uncle Leon was a trucker, therefore I will think cotton.

We stood at the coffin and gazed affectionately at Uncle Leon. His grandson, Craig, who was perhaps about six years old, remarked, "Get away from my grand daddy." I glanced at Craig, who was sitting with his mother, Cousin Angela, and greeted him. Craig then asked his mother, "When is granddaddy going to wake up?" I realized then that Craig, as an adolescent, had not come to the full realization of his grandfather's death.

Some people often comment that the deceased is sleeping or in a state of slumber, therefore some younger children are not fully knowledgeable of the consequences of death.

Days after Uncle Leon's funeral, I visited Aunt Shirley's house and found Craig openly mourning the loss of his grandfather. It is very heart rendering to see the very young mourn the loss of a parent or grandparent. Even now, I remember how Craig and Uncle Leon loved each other as grandson and grandfather. Uncle Leon would often play roughly with Craig during my visits to his home. I often saw Uncle Leon look admiringly upon Craig and his two other grandchildren, who were Cousin Nicole's children.

Towards the end of Uncle Leon's wake, I spied a middle age man, who was dressed in denim clothing, wearing a billed cap and western style boots, walking into the chapel of the funeral home. He walked up to Uncle Leon's coffin and peered in. The trucker then walked out without saying anything to anyone. Uncle Leon's daughter, Nicole, a young lady just barely over twenty years old, asked me if I knew the individual. I told her that he appeared to be a trucker from his manner of dress. She rushed after the man and returned to tell me that she spoke with the stranger and he was in fact a trucker.

There was a slender young man with blonde hair and barely over twenty years of age at the wake. He sat on a bench behind me at the chapel of the mortuary. The young man commented that he I was a relative of Uncle Leon's because of the family resemblance. He seemed sad about Uncle Leon's death and commented that Uncle Leon had taught him how to drive big rigs. The young man praised Uncle Leon for being a good driver trainer, and I thanked him for the compliment.

When we returned to my house from the wake, I received a phone call from Cousin Howard that he was about eight miles from my house and on the main road. He was driving a mini van and had eight other family members with him. I then departed my house at Chesterfield County, Virginia, located my relatives on the main road and guided them to my house.

Upon our arrival at my house, my relatives disembarked from

their mini van. With several of my relatives steadying her, Granny, who is Uncle Leon's mother, slowly ascended the steps of my colonial home and sat on a sofa in the den. Granny appeared solemn, but as the matriarch of our family, she displayed courage despite the circumstances of her visit. I recalled this as being one of her few trips away from her home state or North Carolina. It was ironic that Granny was making such a visit, because Uncle Leon had told her during the past that he wanted her to see the house that he had bought in Virginia. It was incredulous that Granny, who was almost one hundred years old, had the stamina and determination to come to her son's funeral

Granny spied my big screen television, chuckled loudly and commented that my television was large enough for easy viewing. She was also impressed with the size of my house and commented that I had enough room to accommodate many relatives. My wife Ruth had cooked a boneless ham, a turkey and several side dishes in advance. My first cousins (Andrea and Evette and their adolescent children), my nephew (Jermaine), my sister (Helen) and an aunt (Virginia) took a tour of my house. I showed them the various rooms were they would sleep for the night. My first cousin (Howard) and his adult son sat at the dinette table and my wife placed plates of food before them for their consumption. Cousin Howard and his son smiled broadly and began devouring their food. Cousin Andrea's daughter (Kristina), who was elementary school age, looked with interest at my black and white Border Collie dog (Bridget) and at Sam our hair shaven orange colored Persian cat. With his closely shaven hair, Sam resembled a cat that had played in a comical animated feature, which I could not recall the title of at the time.

The gas log flickered with roaring flames in the fireplace of the den while Granny watched the big screen TV intently. I stole a glance at Granny and marveled at her longevity. I was also saddened by the fact that I was unable to do anything to prevent the accident that claimed Uncle Leon's life. This was an issue that had been nagging at me since his death and I consoled myself with the fact that some deaths can not be prevented. As always, a combination of events sometime result in someone's demise. In my opinion, the initial event was my uncle's decision to train drivers and then drive as a team with them.

The day of Uncle Leon's funeral, my relatives awakened during the early morning hours and my wife and I prepared a hearty breakfast for them. Granny eyed me strangely and gave me a scowl as she saw me frying eggs, bacon and other foods for breakfast. Being that she is from the old school, Granny felt that men should not be in the kitchen cooking and that the kitchen was a woman's domain. Women relatives of my family devote idle gossip time to talking about the men relatives of the family who had wives that could not cook. This was not true of the situation with my wife, who was reared in South Carolina, and can cook hearty southern meals. My wife could easily consume leftovers from supper for breakfast. In Ruth's opinion, any edible food can be breakfast. After our marriage, Ruth discovered that her strapping husband desired a plate of grits, fried eggs, sausage or bacon and toast for breakfast. On occasions, Ruth would prepare my favorite breakfast, but the majority of the time, I would simply prepare it myself.

When I was eight years old during 1963, I was cooking simple meals because my ailing mother was often hospitalized. My mother showed me how to cook simple recipes. I cooked other things by reading the preparation instructions on the foodstuff. I was an asset to my father, who was often forced to cook our meals when he returned home from work.

Three pounds of bacon, 1 pound of grits, three dozen eggs, and three gallons of orange juice were devoured by my thirteen relatives, Ruth and I. After breakfast, we dressed in the customary dark mourning apparel and prepared to depart home for Uncle Leon's funeral services.

A short time later, we departed our colonial styled house in two mini vans and drove to the mortuary.

Conscience: "Wait a minute Willie. You are not telling this story the way that it happened. You left out what happened last night while you were sleeping. Hey Willie, if you are going to leave out important events, then you should just quit all together." I then responded to the voice, "Okay, do not be so picky."

I was jerked back to reality as my wife Ruth walked into my computer room. Ruth asked, "Bill, who are you talking to? You better not be on that telephone gossiping." I responded, "No Ruth, I am just talking to myself." Ruth then looked at me quizzically and walked off shaking her head.

The night before the funeral, and into the wee hours of the morning I felt a strange presence in my bedroom. A familiar voice said, " Willie, have some concern for Nicole." I remembered nodding. I then shuddered and went back to sleep.

When we arrived at the mortuary, Uncle Leon was already in the chapel and his coffin was open. My cousin, Howard, pushed Granny, who was sitting in a wheel chair up to Uncle Leon's coffin. Granny sat there in her wheel chair and gazed at Uncle Leon. Her face was saddened and Granny slightly relaxed and tightened her lower jaw and her eyes appeared wet. Granny sat near his coffin for about ten minutes, but it seemed that she sat there for an eternity. I became concerned and asked Cousin Howard if he should consider moving Granny to the seating area of the chapel. Cousin Howard, who had not displayed any substantial emotion throughout this ordeal, snapped at me that Granny was all right and stormed out the chapel. Cousin William walked after him and consoled him.

Other relatives arrived minutes before the funeral services and began to outwardly wail and grieve. Within minutes, and at the precise time of the funeral service's starting time, a funeral director walked up to Uncle Leon's coffin, hastily removed the American Flag from it, closed the coffin's lid and sealed it shut with a hand crank device. He removed the hand crank from the slotted end of the coffin and covered the coffin with the flag. It appeared that the director did not intend to open the coffin again, though it is customary at our family funerals to open the coffin for a final viewing as the family and friends depart the church before travelling to the gravesite. I surmised that there would be controversy concerning the director's actions.

After the delivery of a sermon by a clergyman and an elegant, but emotional eulogy by Cousin Andrea, the funeral services were concluded.

But before I forget. An elegant lady in a red skirt delivered a reading of Uncle Leon's obituary. Cousin Andrea described during her eulogy how Uncle Leon worked hard all of his life. She described how he was a joy to his whole family and how badly he would be missed. Andrea struggled with her emotions while delivering the eulogy but it appropriately honored Uncle Leon's legacy. The choir then sang a beautiful spiritual song and I could hear many people quietly weeping. There were a substantial number of people at the funeral to include workers and supervisors from the trucking company that employed Uncle Leon.

The funeral director did not open the coffin for a final viewing of Uncle Leon's remains. The director assembled the six pallbearers and they placed Uncle Leon's coffin in a hearse. This is always the toughest time for me, the placing of the coffin in a hearse for the final journey to the gravesite. It was a grim time indeed and the jaws of my face were locked shut. I then moved as if I was in a trance or having a bad dream towards our mini van. My wife, Ruth, clung to my arm and comforted me during the short walk to our van.

With the black and elegant hearse at the head of the motorcade, a long convoy of cars snaked out of the driveway of the mortuary and headed towards the cemetery. A police officer on a motorcycle with siren blaring and blue light flashing proceeded the motorcade and stopped traffic at key intersections to allow the motorcade passage.

Upon the motor procession's arrival at the gravesite, I spied a military honor guard already in place. Friends and relatives then disembarked from limousines and cars and walked towards a tented area at the gravesite. Aunt Shirley, her three daughters and two grand children sat on chairs at the gravesite. Granny, who was stooped with age, and assisted by family members, began her snail like approach to the gravesite. She was the last to arrive. The funeral home director then sarcastically commented that Granny could just take her time because we had all day. Taking into consideration, the human array of titans that composed Uncle Leon's immediate family, I surmised that the funeral director was either a brave man or a fool. I concluded that he was the latter. I saw Cousin William, who is a giant of a man, give the director a steely glare. The director, a small man in stature, flinched and then dissolved into the crowd of mourners. Needless to say, patience with the director was wearing thin on all fronts. I shook my head and swore under my breath that there was never a dull moment at our family funerals. Hell, my relatives could raise enough fuss at our funerals without outside assistance. Being that we were all relatives, we could fuss with each other and leave intact, but an outsider would most likely be in need of medical attention.

Despite the funeral director's impatience, the graveside services began only after Granny was seated. Well, Granny brought Uncle Leon into this world and in my opinion she ranked as the most important person there. Besides, Granny had given birth to eight other children and that triples the respect that I have for her.

All of the attendees present were humbly silent as the military honor guard folded the American Flag and presented it to Aunt Shirley. She then walked up to Uncle Leon's closed coffin and placed her hand tenderly on top of it. This was one of the hardest things that I had to cope with that day. Dressed mournfully in black, Aunt Shirley symbolized the many widows without husbands.

The widow who inspired me the most when I was an adolescent and eight years old was Mrs. Jacqueline Kennedy. I sat with my eyes glued to the television set during November 1963 after the assassination of President John F. Kennedy. I watched television for sixteen hours a day until the burial of JFK. I saw Mrs. Kennedy filled with sorrow, but regal, attending the funeral services for her husband.

I have always felt that the death of a man brings grief to his blood relatives, but it is heart wrenching to see a man's lone widow at his burial. Marriage is an institution but the bonding of a man and a woman as mates has even a greater significance. It embodies love, passion, sharing, and mutual respect between two people. The lone widow is a painful reminder of that union, and Mrs. Jacqueline Kennedy carried her husband's memory elegantly after he was gone.

I learned from my uncle's supervisors, who were at the funeral that my uncle's truck did not slide off a mountain. It happened that the trainee truck driver might have fallen asleep while driving on an interstate in the valley near Pulaski, Tennessee. My uncle was sleeping in the sleeping compartment of the truck. The truck went off the roadway at a bridge and traveled about ninety feet down an embankment into four feet of water. The trailer of the truck, which was carrying twenty-five thousand pounds of air conditioners crashed over onto the top of the tractor's cab and totally demolished it. The trainee was discovered in the driver's seat and my uncle in the sleeping compartment. Later, I spoke with a Tennessee Highway Patrolman, who investigated the accident at the scene and he confirmed everything that I was told.

After the conclusion of my uncle's graveside services, the motorcade followed the limousine, which bore Aunt Shirley and her daughters, and was driven by the funeral director. The director at times exceeded the speed limit by thirty miles per hour while traveling to Aunt Shirley's house. I had planned to have a chat with the director back at Aunt Shirley's house, but upon my arrival, the director had dropped off Aunt Shirley and her family. He sped off in the limousine. I surmised that this director did not visit with families after funerals to eat a snack, show his concern for the mourners and make contacts for future business. His rationale must have been that since people are always dying, the funeral business will never be at a lull. I can say wholeheartedly that his funeral home will never get any business referrals through me.

Conscience: *"Well, it's a good thing that Cousin Earl was not at the funeral. May he rest in peace. Earl would have given that funeral director a piece of his mind. That's for sure honey."*

I exited my mini van upon arriving at Aunt Shirley's house, and I saw Granny, who was assisted by several of my other relatives, walking slowly towards the house. Granny looked at the two-story colonial style house that Uncle Leon had bought and openly appraised it with a warm smile on her face.

Upon entering Aunt Shirley's home, I observed that numerous platters of food were laid out for the reception after the funeral. Aunt Shirley, who seemed distraught after her husband's funeral services, was maintaining her composure and graciously greeting attendees at the reception.

Aunt Shirley had decided that she would socialize with relatives and friends during the reception, but she would also be thankful for their departure later. The events of the day had drained Aunt Shirley emotionally and she was looking forward to resting after the ordeal. Granny and Uncle Leon's other relatives extended their condolences to Aunt Shirley and invited her to visit them at North Carolina. I ate at the reception and then informed Aunt Shirley that I was departing for the drive home with my wife. Aunt Shirley was reluctant for me to leave so soon, because she had relied upon me to assist her during her time of grief. I assured Aunt Shirley that I would visit her the next day and reminded her that many things still needed to be accomplished to settle Uncle Leon's estate. Ruth

31

hugged Aunt Shirley and then we departed the reception for our drive home.

Since most of my relatives were staying over at my house for a second night, we made more preparations when we arrived home to accommodate them. My relatives would be returning to my home after the reception.

My relatives arrived at my home after the reception and as the gas log in my fireplace kept the house comfortably warm, they conversed about Uncle Leon with fond memories of him. There was an occasional laugh as some relatives recalled some of the mischievous things that Uncle Leon did during his lifetime.

I recalled one of Uncle Leon's exploits were he placed a harness on a huge white sow or female hog that was lazing in her pen. The sow took Uncle Leon for a wild ride. It tried frantically to scrape him off her back by rubbing him against the fencing of the pigpen as the sow grunted and ran. Uncle Leon, who was riding the sow rodeo style, was hooting and hollering. His ride came to a dramatic conclusion when he fell off the sow's back and she stepped onto his abdomen. The sow's four hundred plus pounds of bulk caused Uncle Leon to double over in pain.

Granny sternly admonished Uncle Leon. With her voice raised to a husky and raspy pitch, Granny's scolding of Uncle Leon was replete with, "You crazy thing. You know better than to ride that sow. A good thing that she did not kill you. You children just worry me to death. And the rest of you children standing there, get out of this house!" Granny eyes flashed, but she moved quickly to examine Uncle Leon's injury, where the sow's hoof had scratched the skin on his belly. Granny then paused momentarily and went to get some of her homemade ointments. Granny's homemade ointments were always fast healing because she mixed them at full strength. Granny had a variety of homemade remedies for colds, measles, punctures of the skin and congestion.

On occasions, I would trudge behind Granny as she ventured

into the woods near the farm to collect sassafras plant roots to boil and create a delicious smelling tea. I would feign a sore throat or congestion on occasions to get a sip of sassafras tea. Granny would chuckle and fill up a cup for me. Granny would then slyly ask if the sassafras tea was working, and would quip that perhaps some Castor Oil was needed. I would hurriedly say that I was cured and bolt out the door.

Granny filled small leather bags with a mixture of raw turpentine, kerosene, rubbing ointment and who knows what else and tied them around one's neck to relieve nasal congestion. The bag would release strong fumes that would clear up nasal congestion, but the bag on one's chest would peel the skin below it.

There was always interesting thing occurring at my grandparents' farm during the times when I was five years old. It seemed that I was often attacked by some of the farm animals.

One day I was standing in the farmyard, and I was suddenly struck from the rear on the buttocks. I turned around and there was a small goat standing behind me. The goat had its head down and was eating some hay off the ground. I was befuddled and in my childish mind, I could not comprehend who or what had struck me. I turned to walk away and was struck from behind again. I peered back to the rear of me and saw that the goat had moved forward from where he had been eating hay. I then surmised that the goat had butted me from behind. I then recalled seeing a cartoon on television when a goat butted someone from behind.

During the late nineteen fifties, there were black and white televisions, and color televisions were unheard of. I would watch Channel Six, WECT, which was the only channel that was available for viewing. The positive thing about having one television channel was that there were never any arguments about which channel we would watch. My favorite show back then was Bonanza with Lorne Greene, Michael Landon, Dan Blocker, and Pernell Roberts. They were the Cartwrights and starred in a western that showed each Sunday evening at about seven o'clock. Bonanza was a very popular television show, and I often saw episodes of it being shown on television back during the early nineteen nineties. I even viewed Bonanza on German television back during the nineteen seventies and eighties. It was interesting hearing the Cartwrights speak the German language on television, as the series were sound dubbed in German. "Ja Hoss, das ist richtig." I translate this to mean, "Yes Hoss, that is right."

I then yelled at the goat and pursued it through the farmyard and towards the tobacco field. Well, the goat easily outran me and I walked back towards my grandparents' house rubbing my smarting and tender posterior.

Of course, no barnyard is complete without a rooster or the barnyard pimp. Granny owned a bright red rooster, which use to strut around the barnyard like an army general marching in review of his soldiers. The rooster strutted around the barnyard with his head held up high and every step he took seemed precise. It seemed that the rooster would stop and often glare at me, therefore I always kept my distance.

However, on one unfortunate day, I felt air rushing towards the back of me and sharp talons struck the back of my head. The rooster was flying in the air and delivering an airborne attack upon my person. The rooster was cackling madly and my legs went immediately into super drive. I kept running until I could hear no more flapping wings. After this particular excursion, I kept my distance even further from the rooster and never turned my back on him.

Several months after the rooster attacked me, I did not see him around the barnyard on one particular day. I went into my grand parent's house and smelled chicken and dumplings boiling. Granny was humming and greeted me as I walked inside the house. She adoringly quipped, "How you doing bright eyes?" I smiled shyly, and bashfully asked Granny about the whereabouts of the rooster. She pointed towards the covered pot that was boiling on top of her natural gas stove. Granny stated that the rooster would be joining us for supper. I smiled inwardly, knowing that one of my adversaries was now being cooked up for supper. Granny also explained that old roosters are tough birds and that only boiling make them tender enough for consumption. Granny explained that a hen is always tender for consumption and perhaps a rooster when it's fairly young. Well, to make a long story short, the rooster was rather delicious, and I even had seconds.

Of course, as time progressed, the goat, which butted me, was also slaughtered. I then found that slaughtering a goat produces some very offensive odors. I stood a mile away during its slaughter and could still smell the goat. On days that Granny stewed up goat meat, I refrained from eating the meat. Those were my vegetarian diet days.

Before we retired for the night, I commented about Uncle Leon's willingness to take risks, hoping that my relatives would acknowledge that Uncle Leon lived his life the way that he wanted. In the end, we all agreed that Uncle Leon did what he desired, regardless of anyone else's opinions and advice. We then honored Uncle Leon for being a part of our lives and for the many things that he contributed to our family.

Chapter Four

A Period of Mourning

(1997)

The next morning, I bade Granny and the other relatives goodbye as they departed for the drive back to their homes in North Carolina. It was ironic that the occurrence of an event like my uncle's death had caused frail Granny to visit my home. I doubted that she would ever have visited my home during her lifetime otherwise.

Though my heart yearned to be at North Carolina with my blood relatives, my travels had brought me to Virginia. It was strange concerning how I came to live at Virginia. I was stationed near Frankfurt, Germany but owned a house near Fort Bragg, North Carolina where I had spent eleven years of my twenty-year army career. Upon my departure from Germany, my military orders assigned me to Fort Pickett, Virginia. Fort Pickett came under the military command at Fort Bragg and was a post with training facilities. When I arrived at Fort Pickett, I was sent to Fort Bragg to in process, and I could have requested a transfer from Pickett to a military unit at Fort Bragg. Then, I could have moved back into my house. I am superstitious to some degree, therefore I have never changed my military assignments. In my opinion, the assignments represented my future fate and destiny. "Woe be to him who tries to change his fate." The icing on the cake was that Uncle Leon lived in Virginia. It happened that I bought a house about fourteen miles from where Uncle Leon lived and adjacent to the same major highway as his home. However, I did not know where Uncle Leon lived at in the nearby city when I purchased my house in Virginia. Perhaps it was all coincidental.

I met with Aunt Shirley several days after Uncle Leon's funeral. She commented that Uncle Leon never allowed her to work and he was always the breadwinner. Aunt Shirley, who was dressed sorrowfully in dark clothing, then looked at me sternly. Aunt Shirley is the kind of lady who is straightforward and direct to the point and the seriousness of her facial expression communicated this to me. Aunt Shirley then remarked that she had told Uncle Leon to get rid of his trainee and I surmised at that point that she never liked his trainee. I looked at Aunt Shirley quizzically and she elaborated that Uncle Leon had apprised her of the trainee's bad driving habits and problems with an estranged wife. It seemed that Aunt Shirley was now going through the guilt stage associated with the loss of a loved one, especially when she remarked that she did not force Uncle Leon to make all of the hauling trips he was reputed for. I spoke to Aunt Shirley in a comforting way, telling her I knew how ambitious my uncle was. I reminded her that we needed to complete insurance death benefit papers, and that Aunt Shirley would have to consult with an attorney about workman compensation benefits as Uncle Leon was killed on the job.

Cousin Bridget, who is Uncle Leon's daughter walked into the room and gave me a gruff greeting. Typical of my blood relatives, Bridget is tall, big boned, and intelligent. I often joke that the majority of my family members could be the starting tackles for professional football teams. Bridget, who was about sixteen years old, kicked a hole in the wall of her home after hearing of her father's death. Aunt Shirley then apologized for Bridget's demeanor. Bridget knew that I was there to assist with the settling of her father's estate. My being there only brought additional confirmation that her father was gone. I gazed at Bridget in a comforting way and silently asked her to trust me. Her facial expression softened and she politely excused herself.

I have always felt strange when visiting Aunt Shirley's house, even when Uncle Leon was alive. It seemed that I was stepping into a time portal and being transported back to the eighteen hundreds. It's because of the rigid way that Aunt Shirley presents herself. Since she is the wife of my youngest deceased uncle, she is no more than ten years older than I. Aunt Shirley is a frequent attendee at church and travels daily to conduct evangelist activities for her church. However, her Christian religious denomination does not have the strictest rules, when compared to the Amish and the Mennonites. I am always astounded by the behavior of her lovely daughters, who are my cousins. Though they are of adult age, they will scurry up the stairs of the house and stay away from houseguests, especially men guests. It is symbolic of the days of old, where families were protective of the women until they married. My grandparents reared two sons and seven daughters. All seven daughters acquired husbands, which seemed in keeping with the strict standards that were employed by my grandparents.

My grandfather or "Pa Daddy" was faced with the dilemma of having seven daughters, but they were sturdy .He could get a complete day's work out of them. In some cases, his daughters were more efficient than some men field hands that he hired for a couple of days during harvesting season. Pa Daddy knew that female children could be useful as workers until they bore children. Afterwards, they would be more occupied with raising children than toiling in the fields during the extremely hot southern summers. His objective was for his daughters to marry as young adults. It happened that since Pa Daddy reared nine children, of whom were born several years apart, he had several grandchildren that were the same ages as Pa Daddy's youngest daughters and son. Theoretically, Pa Daddy benefited from the arrangement, even after several of the daughter's marriages failed and they returned to his farm. Ultimately, his older daughters, who returned, provided him with grandchildren that he employed as laborers.

I could see some of Pa Daddy's legacy at Uncle Leon's house, because it seemed that Uncle Leon's daughters were schooled in the old fashioned etiquette from years long past.

My rambling thoughts ceased, when Aunt Shirley stated, " Willie, Leon was always worried about you. Especially because you are a police officer." Aunt Shirley then paused and looked at me ruefully. She then stated, "Leon told me that he was psychic, but if he was, why is he dead now?" I smiled at Aunt Shirley and politely shrugged my shoulders.

I then sat down with Aunt Shirley to carefully review and complete some documents relative to my uncle's death. I then recalled an old adage, which says you bury your dead and then go on with the activities of life. I then thought, "The living have to go on living", as I filled out volumes of death claim forms.

Later, as I rode in my pickup truck towards home, I reflected on Aunt Shirley's comments about Uncle Leon being psychic. In my opinion, some people do have psychic abilities. Scientists have proven this. There are various levels of psychic abilities. Some people had dreams that materialize. Others can be awake and see premonitions of things to come. In the scheme of things, even though people may have psychic abilities, I doubt they can see the date of their own demise. It seems that the goddesses of fate, which are mythological of course, but even better, some divine force gives some people a glimpse of the future or what will be. However, it seems that these abilities are rationed out sparingly and only a divine power knows the date of anyone's final fate or destiny.

I recalled during the late nineteen nineties when Mike Tyson was released from prison. He had a boxing bout shortly thereafter on pay television with a badly matched opponent. My Uncle Leon came to my house to watch the match with my wife and I. It happened that my sister in law, Jean, from New York City stopped by our residence while travelling south. I recalled that she was either travelling to or from Cheraw, South Carolina, which is her hometown. Jean a statuesque woman arrived before the showing of the boxing match, I introduced her to Uncle Leon. We then saw an advertisement on the television about the psychic connection. Uncle Leon stated that he was psychic. My wife, Ruth, and Jean chuckled at his comments. I smiled and purposely made no comments. Uncle Leon then invited Jean to sit at my dining table for a palm reading. Uncle Leon then plucked at his bulbous nose, and then had Jean lay her hand on the table palm up. He studied her palm tentatively and my wife, Ruth, giggled. Uncle Leon then announced, "Jean you have a friend named Frank." Before Uncle Leon could continue, Jean exclaimed, "That is correct and how do you know that?" My wife's facial expression then became serious, because Uncle Leon had made a correct statement. Uncle Leon studied Jean's palm again and exclaimed that he sees her in a medical place and working with people. Jean was shocked, and stated, " I am a phlebotomist. I take blood samples from people for testing." Uncle Leon's revelations came as no shock to me. I purposely made no comments about my own experiences. Later, we watched the boxing bout, which was over in about the first round. I exclaimed after the boxing match, "Well, Mike Tyson continues to be the undertaker of boxing. He puts them away fast."

About two weeks after Uncle Leon's funeral, I traveled to the home office of the trucking company that he worked for. Aunt Linda and Uncle Stephanie accompanied me. The safety supervisor, a pleasant man in his fifties, met with us and made complimentary remarks about Uncle Leon's contributions to the trucking company. The supervisor remarked that Aunt Linda and I strongly resembled Uncle Leon. The supervisor then chuckled and recalled that Uncle Leon was painfully bashful, but that Uncle Leon would greet all of the workers at the trucking firm's headquarters during his stops there. He stated that Uncle Leon drove the most miles and was the highest salary earner. The safety supervisor promised that the company would erect a plaque at the company in memory of him. The supervisor commented that the company's safety record had always been good and that they had not suffered a fatality among the drivers in over fifteen years. He mentioned that the truck's logs showed that the drivers operated it properly and took the proper rest breaks. I have heard stories that sometimes truck drivers fudge entries on their travel logs so that they can drive longer than The Department of Transportation dictates.

The safety supervisor escorted us to the parking yard for the big rigs to show us the remains of Uncle Leon's big rig or tractor. I craned my head and neck in an attempt to locate the wreckage as we drove through the parking yard. I was astonished when the safety supervisor stopped at a long trailer with wheels, which was damaged extensively on its sides. I noticed that the huge hitch on the front of the trailer was broken off during the accident and metal rails were welded to the front of the trailer. The metal rails were configured into a temporary hitch that facilitated the towing of the trailer from Tennessee to North Carolina by a tractor. The safety supervisor then opened up the rear door of the badly damaged trailer and I saw a huge badly mangled pile of metal on back of the trailer. I looked at the pile of metal quizzically and glanced at the safety supervisor. He then explained that the pile of metal was the remains of the truck or tractor that my uncle was riding in. I was shocked because the cab of the truck did not resemble anything of the truck that I use to see my uncle drive. The remains of the truck looked like a pile of metal rubble. It was obvious that after the truck left the roadway and went down the embankment, the trailer, which was loaded with about twenty-five thousand pounds of air conditioners, crashed over onto it. While I was examining the remains of the truck, I noticed that Aunt Linda was weeping and leaning on her husband for support. I apologized to them for my lack of sensitivity, because my personal examination of the demolished cab was relative to my police training. I was accustomed to examining demolished vehicles, because I had encountered many at traffic accident scenes.

41

The safety supervisor then escorted us to a maintenance building and the contents of Uncle Leon's truck were neatly stacked in a corner. I spied a pair of western boots that Uncle Leon often wore and recovered them from the other items. My heart swelled with pride because the boots were now a reminder of Uncle Leon and a memento of him. Aunt Shirley had specifically reminded me to recover the boots and some other personal items that belonged to Uncle Leon. I then rummaged through the other items and soiled clothing that Uncle Leon and the other driver had worn. The clothing had a pungent but pleasant odor about them; therefore I experienced a sensory sensation in handling them. *I was searching for something that would show me the past or a time before the crash of the truck.* I continued to search through the personal effects, and I then found a neatly folded handwritten letter.

My hands trembled slightly as I unfolded the letter. I then saw that the driver trainee, who had perished, had written the letter. The letter was addressed to the trainee's estranged wife. He documented their travels across country from five days prior to the accident until the day before the catastrophe. The driver trainee detailed in his letter the daily rigors of being a trucker, and his feelings of loneliness. I did not completely read the letter because it was very personal and heart rendering. I then surrendered the letter to the safety supervisor who was standing nearby and commented that perhaps the letter should be sent to the trainee's estranged wife or family. The letter immortalized the trainee's last thoughts about his life prior to his death. I then pondered whether Aunt Shirley should be told about the letter, because it might not be of any comfort to her.

The safety supervisor later displayed some photographs from the accident scene. One photograph depicted a mangled guardrail that was positioned on the side of the road at the entrance to the bridge. The guardrail was flimsy and the big rig striking it would have been the same as a hand swatting a mosquito. Clearly, if the driver were sleeping, it would have not warned him of the impending danger. It was obvious from the photographs that even if the trainee driver had heard a slight noise, the truck would have already been travelling down the embankment or ravine in a fatal plunge. It was a no way out situation unless a miracle occurred. The crash occurred within a few seconds, after the truck began its plunge, given its speed and weight.

Another photograph depicted the interstate on which Uncle Leon and his trainee had traveled before the crash. The interstate had two lanes travelling in either direction and there was a wide grassy median in the center of the lanes of travel. In fact, the median was wide enough to accommodate two big rigs side by side. The median was continuous with the length of the interstate highway. I then commented to the safety supervisor that it was ironic that the trainee ran off the road right at the bridge because if the truck had run off the interstate before or after the bridge, the median would have spared the truck's occupants. It appeared that the truck could have possibly stopped in the grassy median after the trainee applied the brakes.

The trainee would have been startled by the truck bouncing onto the median and reacted. Theoretically, an attempt to turn the truck's front wheel sharply to get back onto the roadway would have possibly resulted in the truck flipping over onto its side. If time did not permit the turning of the steering wheel, the truck would have careened across the grassy medium and onto the traffic lanes on the opposite side of the interstate. Failure to regain control of the truck at this point would have resulted in it striking the drainage ditch of the interstate. The chances of survival in any one of these scenarios, except crashing down the embankment, would have been greater.

The safety supervisor nodded his head knowingly after my summation. We both then shook our heads with grim faces, because we both knew without saying that luck was not with the drivers that early morning as they traveled the abandoned interstate.

The safety director continued to outline the grim circumstances of the crash. The truck was hidden at the bottom of the embankment after the fatal crash and no portion of it could be seen from the roadway. After the early morning crash, many passenger vehicles crossed the bridge without the passengers realizing that the demolished big rig with its operators lied below the bridge.

When the big rig did not arrive at Nashville, Tennessee at seven o'clock in the morning as scheduled and still did not materialize a couple of hours later, the trucking firm that employed Uncle Leon dispatched another big rig to search for the missing truck. Several hours after the crash, the search vehicle driver spotted the damaged guardrail at the bridge and deep wide tire impressions on the muddy shoulder of the roadway. The trucker then stopped off the shoulder of the road, got out of his big rig and inspected the area below the bridge. He was astonished to find the demolished remains of Uncle Leon's big rig. Shocked, the trucker radioed in his find to the trucking company's dispatcher.

The Tennessee Highway Patrol was notified and dispatched Troopers to the scene. I recalled that the trucker, who discovered the demolished big rig, was at Uncle Leon's funeral. He told us that he had found the wreckage of Uncle Leon's truck and gave us Uncle Leon's driver's license.

During our return drive to Virginia, Uncle Stephanie, who had started driving big rigs with Uncle Leon during the early 1970s made comments concerning the accident. He poignantly explained that most truck drivers at the firm where we had just left would be reluctant to come in contact with the cab of the demolished truck or the contents from it. There seemed to be some superstitious beliefs about touching or disturbing things that were associated with the deceased drivers. Uncle Stephanie also explained that a big rig is equipped with a Jake Brake.

The Jake Brake is designed to assist the braking system on wheels of the cargo trailer and tractor. Uncle Stephanie outlined that the Jake Brake is not attacked to the foot brake in the cab of the truck and is a push button or flip lever device that is engaged to increase the braking of the tractor. The Jake Brake causes the truck's engine to create a vacuum which powers down the truck engine suddenly. It is similar to driving a standard shift car and shifting from fourth gear to third gear in conjunction with using the foot brakes to stop the vehicle more efficient. In actuality, when the engine is forced to gear itself down, the revolutions of the tires are dramatically decreased, and there is increased stopping power. Uncle Stephanie cited the importance of the Jake Brake if a truck ran off the roadway .

According to Uncle Stephanie, more experienced drivers engage the brake to bring the big rigs to a more efficient stop during treacherous road conditions and other situations. He stressed that the alertness of the driver is relative to engaging the Jake Brake at the most optimum time. I have heard big rigs making loud rumbling sounds when coming to a stop. Uncle Stephanie explained that the driver had engaged the Jake Brake, which make the loud sound.

Conscience: *"You need to explain where the truck was travelling from and why Uncle Leon was sleeping in the sleeper and not driving."*

The truck was travelling from Houston, Texas where the drivers had picked up twenty-five thousand pounds of air conditioners. Uncle Leon drove from about four o'clock in the evening until midnight. The driver trainee then drove from midnight until about six o'clock in the morning. The truck was about one hour from its destination or Nashville, Tennessee when it ran off the road and crashed. It was almost an eight hundred-mile trip from Houston, Texas to Nashville, Tennessee. The Tennessee Highway

Patrol concluded that the driver had perhaps fallen asleep. There was no other evidence to support any other theories. I notified the Tennessee Highway Patrol about the driver trainee's letter, but they deemed it insignificant to the accident.

In retrospect, I met my uncle's driving trainee on two occasions, perhaps two months or so before their accident. I do not recall his name, but he was a sturdy built man and had a pleasant manner about him. He visited with Uncle Leon at my house. Uncle Leon told me that the trainee was having some problems with his wife. It seemed that they were separated. The trainee told me that he spent time in the military and was stationed in Germany where he met and married his wife.

On the second occasion, Uncle Leon and his trainee were at the Veterans Affairs Hospital at Richmond, Virginia. Another police officer informed me that someone was looking for me in the main thoroughfare of the hospital. I then spoke with my uncle and the trainee near the merchandise sales store of the hospital. About nine months after Uncle Leon's death, I terminated my job at the hospital and became a state employee.

Later that day, I arrived back at Virginia and drove to Aunt Shirley's house. I gave her Uncle Leon's western boots. Aunt Shirley was thankful and told me that her younger daughter, Bridget would probably wear the boots in honor of her father. Aunt Shirley seemed listless and then she sat down. She then looked at me with a mournful look on her face and commented, "I hope that Leon did not suffer." It was a heart wrenching comment; therefore I was forced to pause and steady my own emotions. I then skillfully commented, "No, Aunt Shirley, he did not suffer, because it happened swiftly and Uncle Leon never had any perception of what happened to him." I was able to say this truthfully and with certainty after seeing and inspecting the cab of the truck or what remained of it. I also had an in depth conversation with a Tennessee State Police Trooper about the positioning of the human remains and their appearance after the accident. The remains lacked certain indicators, which supported that Uncle Leon and his driver were not alive for even a split second after the crash. I did not explain the intricacies of this with Aunt Shirley and I never will.

Aunt Shirley then asked if I recovered Uncle Leon's western boots from the cab of the truck. I paused before answering, because there was no way humanly possible for anyone to get into the truck's cab. The cab was a mangled pile of metal and I surmised that most of the items in the cab had exploded outwards when the trailer fell on top of it. The contents of the cab were strewn onto the ground and into the four feet of water that was at the bottom of the ravine. I then skillfully explained to Aunt Shirley that the wreck demolished the cab and the personal items were recovered and stacked inside of a maintenance building. Aunt Shirley then commented that the accident and destruction seemed greater than she had initially thought.

Aunt Shirley then got up from her recliner and retrieved the folded American Flag that was presented to her by the military honor guard at Uncle Leon's funeral. She presented it to me as a keepsake. I knew the day of the funeral that Aunt Shirley would not keep the flag after it was presented to her because of religious beliefs.

. People here on earth have created nations and flags to symbolize them, but certain religious groups feel that there is but one nation and that is the nation of God. I humbly accepted the flag from Aunt Shirley and told her that I would take it with most haste to Uncle Leon's mother.

Chapter Five

The Symbolic Return Home

(1959-1997)

Three weeks after Uncle Leon's funeral, I traveled to North Carolina and presented Uncle Leon's folded U.S. Burial Flag to Granny. Since Uncle Leon was not buried at home in the family cemetery, the presentation of the flag to Granny symbolized his return home. Granny grasped the flag in her weathered hands and promised that she would keep it in a safe place. With the use of a walker, Granny shuffled along at a snail's pace and sat down on a flowery rocker-recliner chair. With her black hair pushed to the rear of her head and the front slightly fringed with slight wisps of white hair, Granny's appearance did not belie the fact that she was over ninety-five years old. Granny then looked at me intently with loving eyes that glowed with inner strength. Granny then commented, " Leon was always a good son. He worked hard and was a good provider for his family." When Granny says it, it's the truth and she not saying it because she brought Uncle Leon into this world.

Granny comes from a strong stock of people, who owned considerable amounts of land and farmed tobacco as a cash crop from the time of the Proclamation Emancipation until the 1970s. Since my granny was born right after the beginning of the twentieth century or the year 1900, she as a child met some of her older relatives, who were slaves before the emancipation proclamation. Granny knows a wealth of stories about slavery times from conversing with the former slaves.

I remembered that during 1971, when Granny was nearly seventy years old, she worked with me one Saturday in the tobacco field. She was a stout and very sturdy woman. Granny worked near the tobacco barn and tied broad green leaves of sandy and sticky tobacco onto long narrow sticks with long pieces of white twine. Granny removed the tobacco leaves from a wheeled cart that was pulled through the tobacco field by a farming tractor. When the carts were filled with tobacco leaves, a farmer would pull the cart to the barn and unhitch it from the tractor. Women would remove the leaves from the carts and tie the tobaccos onto long slender sticks or poles. Granny wore her customary wide brim straw hat, which was anchored on her head, and tied, at her chin with a security string. Granny's hands worked fast and skillfully as she tied three-four leaves of tobacco on one side of the stick and then looped the twine over to the other side of the stick and tied several leaves of tobacco there. When the stick was completed, it had tobacco leaves tied in a neat arrangement on both sides of the stick with no gaps or spaces. Later, men would hang the sticks of tobacco horizontally on the rafters of a tobacco barn for curing by gas heaters. The cured tobacco leaves would later turn brown and crispy and similar to dried tobacco in cigarettes. Granny worked continuously and effortlessly in the ninety-five degree heat.

I was engaged in harvesting the tobacco and broke broad leaves of tobacco off the bottom of the tobacco stalks. I worked stooped over and broke the leaves off the stalks and place them under the arm of my free hand. After moving forward from stalk to stalk, my arm would become filled with tobacco leaves and I would walk a short distance to the wheeled cart and tractor and throw the leaves in. I would then go back to the rows of tobacco and begin cropping tobacco again. The hot sun beamed down on me as I toiled. I sweated profusely between the rows of tobacco leaves because the leaves blocked the cool breezes of air from me.

Cropping tobacco on foot was more tedious than working on a tobacco harvester. I had worked on a tobacco harvester before. Usually four women work on the top covered platform of the harvester, which is about seven feet above the ground. I would ride low to the ground on a contraption resembling a bicycle seat with forward foot pedestals for my feet. I would crop leaves of tobacco from the stalks as the motorized harvester progressed slowly up the field.

I placed the tobacco leaves onto a rotating conveyor chain with grasping clasps. The conveyor chain with grasping clasps then hauled the tobacco leaves to the top of the tobacco harvester's platform where four women, one per cropper, worked. The term "cropper" is pertinent to a person who tears leaves from a tobacco stalk with his or her hands.

The women on the platform above the croppers would grab the tobacco leaves off the rotating conveyor chains when they reached the top of the platform and at waist level. The rotating conveyor chains rotated close to the outer edges of the platform that the women were standing on, therefore the leaves were easily within their reach. The empty clasps would then rotate to the bottom of the harvester, where I would place more leaves between the pulley wheels of the spring loaded clasps.

There would be two other men and my teenage brother, George, riding on platforms similar to mine and placing tobacco leaves on the grasping clasps of the conveyor chains. The rotating chains with grasping clasps were similar to bicycle chains and rotated mechanically in front of the workers like a Ferris Wheel.

Granny worked the whole day near the barn on her feet. She smiled and joked with the other women. Some women were fifty years younger than Granny. I spied Granny at times tying the leaves of tobacco and she appeared intent about her work. I caught myself smiling and thinking that Granny's presence at Little Big Horn with her wide straw hat, stern appearance, and flashing eyes would have caused even Chief Sitting Bull some concerns. I think that this best describes Granny's determination and strength, but she is quick to turn that gruff appearance into a soft and warm smile. Granny could melt ice on a cold winter's day with her smile, followed by a slap across one's back and her cheery laugh. Granny reared nine children and she had lived to attend the funerals of four of them.

Other families besides mine have experienced deaths and tragedies also. However, besides her four children who had died, Granny has a daughter who has been ill for forty years and in a nursing home. This particular daughter is my mother, Annie. Her eldest son, John, was injured in a truck roll over and badly injured when he fell down a flight of stairs about thirty some years prior to Uncle Leon's death. Granny is now left with only three children out of nine whom are fully functional. It can be surmised that the fate of her children has not been the best.

I know the Kennedy family has suffered a lot and I have heard comments made about the Kennedy curse. Taking into consideration, all of the superstitions that are generated in the south, it goes without saying that similar comments have been made concerning our family.

While I conversed at length with Granny, I spied my Uncle John driving up to Granny's old house. Granny was residing with a daughter near her old house, which Uncle John had turned over to his sons to manage. I excused myself and walked over to Granny's house to see Uncle John. I noticed that Uncle John drove his car close to the front porch of Granny's house, which was a wooden structure, covered with green siding.

The best way to describe Uncle John would be to picture the Reverend Jesse Jackson, who my uncle bears a strong resemblance to. My Uncle Leon was slightly shorter than Uncle John but resembled Reverend Jesse Jackson also. Uncle John greeted me from the driver's seat of his car and commented he was going to go inside the house to check on some remodeling that had been done. Uncle John then opened his car door and painstakingly lowered him self from the car into a kneeling position on the ground. He was near a porch rail and grasped it with his right hand and pulled himself forward across the ground until he was lying face down on the bottom steps in a slight kneeling position with the upper torso of his body raised. I noticed the tenacious grips that Uncle John had on the rails of the porch as he continued to pull himself up the stairs and onto the porch. Uncle John rebuffed my suggestions that I help him. He then commented that he had perfected this system for getting upstairs because his legs, as a result of pervious injuries, had failed him several years earlier.

The story goes that Uncle John was riding in a truck with another individual during the 1950s and the truck was involved in a serious accident. The truck rolled over and Uncle John received some minor injuries. During the 1960s, Uncle John was living in an apartment at Durham, North Carolina with his wife and children. He fell down a flight of stairs onto a concrete landing. Uncle John was hospitalized at Duke Medical Center, North Carolina, where he was treated for broken legs and arms. Some of his limbs suffered multiple fractures and he was reassembled with a mass of metal pins, nuts and bolts. Uncle John told me that he went through prolonged therapy to learn how to perform life functions with the limited maneuverability of his damaged limbs.

I know that Uncle John mastered the functions of shooting long guns without being able to bring the aiming sights to eye level. I saw him shoot down wildlife, whether it was airborne or on foot by shooting from the hip. I was skeptical when I first saw him shoot a stray dog that was attempting to predatorize our chicken house. The dog was running fast and a considerable distance away when he fired at it with a rifle. I heard a yelp but the dog kept running and never broke a stride. I told Uncle John that he obviously missed the dog because it kept running and did not drop. He advised me to take a shovel and a long hike up the field. I did and I was never skeptical of his shooting abilities again.

My grandfather or Pa Daddy was also very skilled at shooting long guns and shotguns. Aunt Linda, who is Pa Daddy's youngest daughter, told me about an incident that occurred during the late nineteen fifties. According to Aunt Linda, a hawk or large predatory bird visited the farm. Hawks are notorious for attacking chickens and consuming them. Pa Daddy discovered the hawk, which was perched high in a tree and obtained his shotgun from the house. Pa Daddy cocked the hammer of the shotgun and took aim to shoot the hawk, but the catch or spring on the gun's hammer and trigger mechanism was bad. The hammer on the shotgun flew forward on its own without Pa Daddy touching the trigger. Pa Daddy's hand was near the breach of the gun when the hammer fell. The hammer injured Pa Daddy's hand and ignited the shotgun shell. Pa Daddy did not have the gun's sights on the hawk, therefore the blast from the gun only struck some tree limbs and leaves. The hawk then flew away swiftly, and Pa Daddy noticed that his hand was cut and bleeding from the hammer of the shotgun striking it.

When I had finished telling Uncle John about Uncle Leon's accident, he did not talk about not attending Uncle Leon's funeral. Since Uncle John did not make any comments, I decided not to discuss it. I concluded that perhaps bad health kept him from attending. I learned years ago not to ask Uncle John questions about sensitive issues because he might give you a truthful answer that might seem insensitive. However, his response would be his true feelings. Uncle John commented that his brother, Leon, always boasted of having a large life insurance policy on himself in the event of his demise. I told Uncle John that Uncle Leon had left a sizeable estate and that I was encouraging his wife to get his estate settled. Uncle John commented that if his wife, Aunt Shirley, was in no hurry to settle the estate, that he could take it off her hands. I looked at Uncle John but could not determine if he was serious or just joking.

Uncle John then began to talk about the late 1940s and 1950s and about his father or my grandfather. Uncle John commented that Uncle Leon was like their father in some ways and this is why Grandfather allowed Uncle Leon to do less work than his other eight siblings. Uncle John mentioned that there were many Saturdays when Grandfather or "Pa Daddy" had him and his siblings harvesting tobacco and other crops, but Uncle Leon would be heading to town for a date. Uncle John commented that Grandfather would let Leon go to town and not do his share of the work, and that no one would raise an issue about it. Uncle John's story caused me to remember comments I had heard from my mother and her other siblings concerning their father. It seemed that my grandfather was a strict disciplinarian and his children toiled long and hard harvesting crops in the fields under his supervision. Uncle John did not appear upset about how Uncle Leon skipped out on chores, but he did not seem too pleased about it during his recounting of past events. I then laughed to myself and knew how Uncle Leon managed to work less than anyone else did under Grandfather's strict scrutiny.

Uncle Leon was a master at manipulating people and situations. He was very intelligent and also very convincing. Uncle Leon could tell people that he could make a pearl pocketbook out of a sow's ear and they would believe it. Needless to say he was very mischievous and cunning.

Uncle Leon use to build rabbit boxes when he was a teenager. He would use the boxes to trap rabbits and sell them to people in the surrounding county. I surmised that people might have kept some of the rabbits as pets but I remember them as being a tasty delicacy. Fried or stewed rabbit with the appropriate side dishes was tasty. I would go with Uncle Leon to assist him in sitting up the boxes in the woods near our home. The rabbit boxes or traps were simple but cleverly constructed devices. My uncle would construct the oblong boxes from discarded lumber. The box was completely enclosed except for the front. The front or entrance of the box was open and designed with a slot on the top and bottom of the entranceway. The door of the trap was a piece of plywood, which was designed to fit in the top of the slotted entranceway. The door of the trap was designed to move freely up and down, which is similar to the animal capture cages that are seen on television's wildlife refuge series. On top of the rabbit box and about two-thirds the box's length from the front to the rear was a hole about the circumference of a soft drink bottle cap. A short length of stick was notched on one side at its middle and inserted into the hole on top of the box. The notched stick was then turned to where it would hook onto the edge of the hole. A piece of twine was attached to the top of the stick. A stick of wood about twelve inches long was attached erect about six inches from the slotted entrance of the trap. The top of the stick was slotted. The door of the trap was raised into its upward position by a string attached to the top edge of the door. The string extended from the top of the trap door, up and over the notch of the erect foot high post and down to the stick or trigger that was wedged inside of the trap. If a person looked through the front entranceway of the rabbit box, they would see the bottom tip of the stick or trigger protruding from the ceiling of the box.

Uncle Leon and I would place a piece of apple or other fruit inside the rear of the rabbit box. The trap was triggered when the rabbit entered the box and moved forward to eat the fruit. The rabbits head or back would knock the tip of the stick forward, release it and the front door would slide down and trap the rabbit inside. Holes were drilled in the sides of the traps for ventilation.

Uncle Leon made fair money selling rabbits to various person, however all business ventures are not without risks. On occasions, Uncle Leon would trap rabbits that were diseased by outbreaks of viruses within the rabbit population. He could not sell the diseased rabbits to his customers.

It seemed that Uncle Leon got the zest for entrepreneur ventures from my grandfather or his father. Grandfather or "Pa Daddy" always had several sources of income rolling into his hands at any given time. I remembered that Pa Daddy worked at the Turpentine Plant, supervised the planting and harvesting of crops on the family's small farm, sold baked peanuts at work that he harvested from his fields on the lunch hour and was a peddler of produce at the nearby cities on the weekends. Pa Daddy drove his pickup truck loaded with produce through the neighborhoods on Saturdays and sold vegetables and produce to various people.

A story goes that Pa Daddy also fermented wine back during the nineteen forties or fifties, but that source of income was terminated after a surprise visit by the revenuers or county alcohol beverage control agents. Of course, selling illegal liquor was a respectable business occupation back during those times. My Uncle John still has a secret delicious recipe for wild cherry wine. Uncle John does not consume alcoholic beverages and use to make the cherry wine for his guests. The wild cherries can be harvested during the summer time from the cherry trees near the farm.

I remember, as a small child, during the nineteen fifties and nineteen sixties the "Juke Joints" that were nestled up in the woods of the rural counties. None of the Juke Joints had licenses to sell liquor or anything else. The Juke Joints had what we called juke-boxes or big record playing machines that played a variety of plastic records. There was a Juke Joint within walking distance of our family farm. Granny and her older daughters would look with disdain upon the shiny new Chevrolet and Ford cars that would travel up the rutted dirt road pass their houses with their occupants on their way to the Juke Joint. I would hear Granny and her daughters make comments about sinners and their need to redeem themselves.

On occasions, I would see Uncle John harnessing up the mule to do some plowing in the fields. I would stand nearby and watch Uncle John as he placed a padded yoke over the mule's head and push it back until it butted up against the mule's broad shoulders. The yoke had metal rings extending from it and through the rings, Uncle John would attach strong leather straps that extended from the yoke and body harnesses. The shoulders' yoke and body harness maximized the mule's full pulling capacity when long chains and other straps were attached to them. These long chains and straps would extend from the yoke and body harness to a horizontal wooden bar that would drag on the ground at the rear of the mule. A turn plow, tiller with disk wheels or planter/fertilizer distributor could be attached with chains to the horizontal drag bar. As the mule strode forward, the weight of the plow or other implement would cause the rear drag bar to raise up from the ground. The drag bar would be angled downwards at the rear of the mule as it pulled the plow or farming implement through a field.

My grand parents owned a huge mule, which was broad like a Clydesdale Horse but shorter. From my viewpoint, as a five-year-old, the mule was a huge elephant. But before anyone begins to pity the mule for having to drag heavy farm implements around, it must be elaborated that a mule is genetically engineered to be a beast of burden. A mule is a hybrid, in that a female donkey and a sturdy male horse are mated together to give birth to a mule. Since mules are hybrid animals and sterile, you can not mate a mule with a mule to get a mule. It is impossible. I learned years ago that mules were needed for coal mining, because the heavy carts of coal and under-ground conditions would kill a normal horse. A mule, which is similar to a small bulldozer, could survive thirty years or more in the coalmines.

On one particular day, Uncle John perched me on top of the mule. It seemed that I was at the third floor of a building and my short legs did not extend over the mule's sides. I held onto the mule's harness for dear life as it lumbered forward. The massive muscles on its back rippled and it seemed that the whole world was in motion underneath me. I grew frightened, lost my grip on the harness and fell forever until I struck the ground with a thump. Uncle John heard me fall and asked, "How did you fall off the mule?" I shrugged my shoulders and told him that I would just walk the rest of the way to the field.

When we arrived at the field, which had already been tilled, Uncle John, who was standing at the rear of the mule and guiding the plow, controlled the mule with use of the lengthy harness straps.

With a command of "Giddy up mule", he guided the mule by tugging on one of the two head harness straps, to the farthest edge of the field. My uncle had both ends of the harness straps tied together and positioned around his neck, which left both of his hands free to control the two wooden handles that extended upwards from the frame of the metal edge plow. It seemed that the metal portion of the plow, which cuts through the earth looked like a small anchor from a ship but shaped more like a metal shoe that a medieval knight wears. Once the mule and plow were positioned at the edge of the field, Uncle John commanded it verbally to move forward. He steadied the wooden handles of the plow to keep it balanced and upright, as the mule trudged forward and the implement plowed a furrow in the ground. When Uncle John and the mule reached the end of the field, he caused the mule to make a wide turn and he plowed another furrow adjacent to the first. The plow cut open a path wide enough for a man to walk through carefully and piled up high mounds of dirt on either side of the path. The high mounds of dirt that the plow creates on both sides of the furrow are where the seeds, seedlings or small plants are placed during planting. A farming implement that allows seeds to fall onto the rows of mounded earth can distribute the seeds. However, back during the early fifties, the small nursery plants were painstakingly placed onto the rows of mounds by hand. This required a lot of bending and stooping on someone's parts.

Uncle John decided to let me test my hand at plowing. I grasped the handles of the plow and commanded "Giddy up mule." The mule moved forward and the plow created a crooked furrow and tilted badly to the side, because I could not keep it balanced and upright. The weight of the plow and the mule pulling it overwhelmed me. My uncle chuckled and commanded the mule, "whoa". The mule stopped and Uncle John resumed plowing. He told me that I was off to a good start and would get better with more practice and age.

On occasions, I would see Granny with a huge black cast iron cauldron. She would have the cauldron positioned behind her house and a roaring fire would be heating the water in the cauldron. The water would come to a rolling boil and granny would throw in large pieces of lye soap that she made on the farm with animal fat, lye and some other ingredients. Granny would then boil bed linen in the cauldron. The hot water would thoroughly cleanse the white bed linen. Granny would then hang the linen out on clotheslines to dry. After the linen was dried, I noticed that the linen was stiff and it seemed that someone had sprayed liquid starch on the linen and ironed it smooth with a hot iron. The linen also had a strong pleasant odor from the homemade lye soap.

Sometimes, I would see the cauldron full of hot water and Granny would tell Cousin Howard, one of my older cousins, to stay in the vicinity of the cauldron. Granny would then use the hand pump that was situated at the rear of her house and pump a bucket full of cool well water. Granny would then throw the cool well water into the cauldron to reduce the temperature of the boiling water. She would test the temperature of the water gingerly with her finger and order Cousin Howard to remove his clothing and get in the cauldron. Granny believed in godliness and cleanliness. I would caution Cousin Howard that the water still seemed hot, but he would laugh and sit down into the cauldron of water. Grammy would then throw Cousin Howard a large bar of soap. He would then bathe himself.

While sitting in the cauldron or wash pot, Cousin Howard reminded me of the cartoons about witches that showed on television. It seemed that the witches always had a big black cauldron and would be cooking something in it. I noticed that the steam from the water rose around Cousin Howard and dissipated into the air.

Sitting at a distance from the cauldron, in the backyard of the house, was an old white cast iron bathtub. This bathtub was not used for our bathing. It was used to bathe hogs after they were slaughtered. After a hog was slaughtered, which was usually during the late fall prior to the holidays, with much groaning and straining, Uncle John, Uncle Leon and the larger of my male cousins would place the hog in the bathtub. It would be filled with hot water and a strong solution of lye. A hog is covered with a hairy bristle like hide; therefore hogs are not skinned after slaughter like other animals. After the hog lies in the hot lye and water solution for a short period of time, his bristle like hide is softened. Then my relatives would use brushes and scrapers to scrub and scrape the hair off the hog until it was pink and white like a new born baby. Then after more groaning and straining, my relatives would hang the hog by the hind legs from a horizontal rafter that was supported on both ends by large vertical four inch by four-inch sturdy poles. Other relatives would place a huge forty-gallon metal wash pan under the carcass of the hog. I had seen my relatives hang hogs that were three hundred pounds plus from the rafter for dissecting. With a sharp knife and a sturdy hand, Uncle John would skillfully start the disemboweling of the hog. He would start cutting at the top and work his way down the under belly of the hog. In this way, he could control the descent of the hogs massive intestinal tubes into the huge metal pan situated below the hog. The intestines of the hog would be filled with excrement, which accounted for the massive weight of the intestines. In essence, a hog or swine is a garbage disposal, and its intestinal system is designed to handle foods that have reached volatile levels of decay. The only consequence of a hog eating decayed food is a satisfying burp.

My relatives have seen snakes bite hogs. Then the hogs killed the snakes and consumed them. The hogs did not die from the snakes' bites. I guess snake venom is an appetizer for a hog. However, since a hog eats all foods or anything that is thrown to it, one has to be careful when getting into a hog pen to clean troughs and make repairs. Seems that hogs also have a taste for "leg of man".

I know that some people eat hog intestines and they are popularly called chitterlings. It would be more appropriate to change the "c" of this word to a "s". I have seen the intestines emptied, washed out with hot water, cool water, warm water, and washed over and over again to cleanse them for consumption. Despite all of those preparations, chitterlings still have that distinctive odor when they are prepared on a stove for consumption. I have heard that a potato or onion, or perhaps both, when cooked in with chitterlings, help reduce the odor.

I could be a mile from Granny's house and know what was on the supper menu. However, if I was present and saw my women relatives preparing the chitterlings, it would be a vegetarian diet for my supper that day.

I am not going to go into the sordid details of how our women relatives cleaned the hog intestines. However, an old adage that says, "People eat all of the pig, from the rooter to the tooter" is correct.

Granny was knowledgeable of all aspects of meat preservation. After the slaughter of a hog, time was of essence, to insure that the meat would not spoil. Granny would freeze some portions of the hog in her deep freezer. She had a small smoke house constructed at the rear of her house and with the use of hickory wood, she would place hog meat in the smokehouse and smoke it. This would also preserve the meat for a lengthy period of time. Granny showed me how to take huge containers of raw salt and rub it deeply into the side portions of the hog to make salted fat back. We would rub the salt into the meat deeply on both sides with our hands and then pack the meat in a box of salt for later consumption. The salt would preserve the meat for months. Then I was shown how to mix a salty water solution or brine and soak meat in it over a period of several hours to preserve it also.

Granny had a hand grinder in her storage building and I would see her place choice cuts of lean and fat pork into the grinder and turn the hand crank of the grinder. Shredded pieces of meat that resembled mush would stumble out the bottom of the meat grinder and it would be seasoned and placed into hog intestines or artificial tubes. These were links of sausages, which Granny would either freeze or smoke.

Of course, Granny would give her children, who participated in the slaughter, choice cuts of meat for their own storage and consumption. Nothing on a hog was wasted. I walked into Granny's house one day and a delicious aroma wafted through the air. I noticed a huge dark blue pot with a lid, on top of Granny's stove. I asked Granny what was cooking and she lifted the lid of the pot. I was shocked to see the hog's head in the pot with hot water swirling all around it. It seemed that its eyes were watching me. The water contained seasoning, green peppers, onions, celery and other vegetables. Granny told me that she was in the preparatory stage of making "hog head cheese" or souse meat. Actually, it is a spicy delicacy and I eat souse meat nowadays myself.

One day, my brother George, and I were playing near a fire that Granny had built to burn some refuse. George was three years old and I was five years old. We were running in circles around the fire, when I heard a popping noise. I heard George yell and I noticed that he was bleeding from the temple of his head. I was terrified and looked suddenly in all directions to see who had shot my brother. I ran into Granny's house and summoned her outside, explaining rapidly that something awful had just happened. Granny stanched the bleeding and called my mother by telephone. My mother was working a few miles from our farm at a restaurant. My mother returned home quickly and she and George were transported to a nearby hospital. I was concerned that my brother might die and I waited nervously for their return from the hospital.

Several hours later, my mother returned with George and he had a bandage on the temple of his head. My mother, Annie, explained that a .22 caliber bullet was in the fire that we played near and the fire caused it to ignite and strike my brother on the temple of his head. It happened that the bullet struck one of the hardest portions of his skull, which is located near the side of the head and adjacent to the eye socket. The bullet penetrated his skin and then ricochet.

It was simply amazing that the bullet did not strike my brother or I in a vital area. But like my Granny says, "God works in mysterious ways." Well, after that, my brother and I kept our distance from open fires.

The incident with the bullet striking my brother was the most serious injury that he or I encountered as children. Of course, we suffered other scrapes and bruises around the farm, but Granny was always there with an ointment or potion to heal the wounds. Farms are nice places to be raised at but there are many inherent dangers to children on farms, which have sharp farming implements, farm animals with nasty dispositions, and snakes and other predators that creep out of the nearby woods.

One day, I spied an old black man who was about seventy years old, walking up the road towards Granny's house. He was walking with the use of a walking cane, though it seemed that he did not need one. Granny and Aunt Linda greeted the old man and offered him a seat on the porch of their house. It was during the early summer and it was pleasant and warm outside. I learned that the old man was a friend of my family and that he was famous in some ways. During my recent conversations with Aunt Linda, she identified the old man as "Cousin Matthew", who was related to our family.

It seemed that the old man, whose name I can not recall, was walking home up a deserted road in the rural county one day. For some unknown reason, a bobcat was following him, which is a predatory type animal, the size of huge tomcats. The story goes that the bobcat attacked the old man, who killed it with one blow of his walking cane. I visually inspected the old man's walking cane after remembering this story and saw that it had a heavy engraved metal handle on it. I then concluded that the walking cane in the old man's possession had other uses. I would see the old man from time to time later and he was never without his cane. Without a doubt, he was a man that young thugs would want no dealings with.

Well, who knows if the story of him killing a bobcat was true? Perhaps the bobcat was ill in health and killed easily, but that was never relative to the way the story was told and then repeated. We know that every time a story is recounted, it is slightly embellished. At some point, the bobcat that the old man killed was the biggest bobcat seen in those parts in a hundred years. Of course, the old man was not going to dispute any portion of the stories that had made him a walking legend, so to speak.

After my parents and us siblings moved to live in town or at Wilmington, North Carolina during 1961, we would encounter Granny and Aunt Linda at the supermarket in town. Though it would be Saturday, Granny and Aunt Linda would be dressed in their Sunday best. Granny never departed the farm unless she was dressed immaculately in stylish clothing. Granny, who is short and stout, wore a fancy wide brim hat on her head and thick heel high heel shoes on her feet. She would walk rapidly up the streets to her destinations. Aunt Linda, who was an older teenager, would also be dressed elegantly, but always walking at a distance behind Granny. I believe that my family's feet were never designed for shoes. Most of my family members have our trademark walk, with our toes pointed inward.

Needless to say, regardless if Granny had placed on a brand new pair of shoes off the shelf, the shoes would still look turned over from the rear. I learned from conversations with Aunt Linda that she dreaded Granny wearing high heels, because the shoes always looked pitched over. Aunt Linda explained that this is why she always walked behind Granny at a distance. She did not want her school mates to see her walking with Granny, who would trudge forward swiftly while walking, like an attacking army, with her shoes slightly turned over.

I was always happy to see Granny in town shopping. She always had a few spare coins to give me. Granny would always recount some bad event that had occurred according to the news. She would shake her head and comment that it was just terrible. Granny would use words like "dirty dogs" to describe the persons who had committed certain crimes. She would always close her comments by stating, "What is this world coming to?"

In my opinion, Granny has always thrived to live her life according to strict morals and rules. I have never seen her smoke or consume alcoholic beverages. Undoubtedly, Granny expects other people to be law abiding and decent in their interactions with others. I think that this is the reason why Granny has preferred to live in the rural areas or country all of her life. Rural living is away from the congested cities and it seems that country folk are more endearing and have more respect for their fellow man

I have lived in cities now the majority of my life, but I yearn even now for the sweet smell of blossom trees that line the fields in the country.

I yearn to look upon fertile fields where various crops flourish and smell the odor of vegetation.

To see flocks of birds fluttering overhead against a clear blue sky, and hear the sounds of birds chirping and singing in trees.

I want to drink crisp and sweet water from a well and strode down dusty roads and paths where my ancestors once walked.

Once a person has experienced all of these things, one day he or she will be encouraged to return home to the country.

Chapter Six

My Family's Burden

(1957-1959)

Many families harbor dark secrets and often whisper about them during hushed conversations. One night the wind howled and blew around my grandparent's house, during a time when I was too young to remember. The trees swayed and cast eerie shadows around the house. It all seemed like a dream. I have only vague memories of this time, because I was only two years old. Those memories are similar to cinematic blips and represent dramatic events. It was the month of June during the year 1957. I am two years old and my mother, Annie, is in the hospital, after happening problems with the birth of my brother, George, on 10 May 1957

It seemed that Pa Daddy, my grandfather, was arguing with Granny at their farm. Pa Daddy had flown into a terrible rage after seeing his daughter, Annie, very sick and near death at the hospital. He had instructed his younger daughter, Aunt Della, to stay at the hospital and do what she could to help his son-in-law and his mother.

After returning to the farm, Pa Daddy informed Granny of their daughter's condition. Pa Daddy explained that he had left Aunt Della at the hospital to assist his daughter's husband and mother-in-law.

Pa Daddy then reminded Granny that she and him had received reports during the past that Annie's husband and her mother-in-law, Erdell, were physically abusing her. Pa Daddy reminded Granny that she and him had driven to their son-in-law's house on several occasions to check out the reports of abuse. Pa Daddy stated that though Annie denied that she was being abused, he still suspected that the reports were true.

Pa Daddy remarked that he and Granny had sent their daughter, Della, to live with Annie at the house for several months to assist with her two children. Pa Daddy thought that it was wise to send Aunt Della to help his daughter, Annie, at home, thereby he could obtain accurate information about any abuses.

Pa Daddy then pointed out to Granny that it was already very late at night, and his son-in-law was suppose to have returned Aunt Della home by now. Pa Daddy then pointed out that he was sick and tired of the way that his son-in-law and mother did things. He felt that his daughter's marriage to his son-in-law, William, had been the source of problems.

Granny commented that it was late. She suggested that Pa Daddy retire for the night. Pa Daddy became more conciliatory or it seemed, and stated, "Well, I will just dose off here by the television. I will let you know when our daughter comes home. Helen, you go ahead and get some sleep."

The sky seemed darker that night and the wind more intense than usual. There were dark foreboding clouds in the sky and it seemed a storm was approaching. Suddenly, the porch light was extinguished. The front door of the house creaked. A shadowy phantom crept out and sat on the porch's rocking chair. The phantom sat concealed and veiled in darkness. Suddenly, rolling thunder broke the night's silence and bolts of lightning lit up the sky. As bolts of lightning illuminated my grandparent's house, a metallic shotgun could be seen on the phantom's lap. The rear door of the house was pushed silently open and a shadowy figure with his heart pounding and his luminous eyes wide crept from the rear of the house. He dropped to his knees and then stealthily crawled under the front porch. He cringed and sucked in his breath as the rocking chair creaked back and forth on the timbers of the porch above him. As the chair continued its rhythmic rocking, the person under the porch slowly released his breath and began to breathe quietly.

When things did not appear promising at the hospital, William and his mother, Erdell (my paternal grandmother) decided that they needed to travel to South Carolina. It seemed that Annie's sickness was the result of witchcraft or voodoo. They left Aunt Della in charge of William's and Annie's two children, Helen and Willie, at their house in an adjacent county. Afterwards, William and his mother departed their residence. They stopped before traveling to South Carolina and picked up two other men relatives, William's uncle and cousin. They then traveled to South Carolina.

There they paid a practitioner of the black arts a considerable sum for a talisman that was guaranteed to correct my mother's illness.

My father, William, his mother Erdell, and the two men relatives returned to the house in the adjacent county and picked up Aunt Della, my four year old sister (Helen) and me. My father drove the 1957 Chevrolet and his mother was sitting in the middle of the front seat with my father's Uncle Jesse sitting on the front passenger seat closest to the door. The other occupants of the car were in the back seat. They then proceeded to the adjacent county to drop Aunt Della off at her parent's farm.

The phantom sitting on the rocking chair cocked the shotgun, when he spied a lone car with its luminous headlights pull onto the long dark road that led up to the house. The weakened catch and spring on the cocking mechanism of the shotgun began to creak and groan and the hammer of the shotgun seemed to inch slightly forward on its own. The car continued on towards the house and pulled to a stop in front of it. The several occupants of the car saw the phantom stand up with a shotgun in his hand. They glanced at each other and were confused. Like in a bad dream, the phantom hurried down the steps of the porch. Swearing loudly, he walked to the driver's side of the car and pointed the shotgun at the young man, William. He ordered the young man to get out of the car, but the young man refused. William's mother Edrell, who was sitting in the middle of the front passenger seat, grabbed the barrel of the shot-

gun and tried to wrestle it away from the phantom. The hammer of the shotgun creaked, and the phantom looked down in horror as the hammer of the shotgun flew forward.

Then it seemed that the whole scene outside of the house was now moving in slow motion. My Ancestors from past lives assembled and waited. Atropos, a goddess of fate and destiny checked her scroll and hourglass. She reached for her shears.

The phantom then had a flashback of him trying to shoot a hawk in a tree a couple of months earlier. The phantom saw himself raising the shotgun up to shoot the hawk, but it fired without him pulling the trigger. The phantom then had a sudden realization and a sinking feeling in the pit of his stomach.

The phantom's attention was then suddenly thrust back into the situation at hand. Frantically, the phantom reached at the falling hammer of the shotgun and it gouged a chunk of flesh from his finger. He watched in dread as the hammer slammed forward and ignited the shotgun shell with a thunderous explosion. It broke the dead silence of the night. The pretty lady then sagged sideways against the window and door of the car. The front of her dress was red like a robin's breast. The shotgun shell had struck her abdomen. The wind whistled and howled as she entered into eternity. Atropos had cut her thread of life.

I was awakened from my dream by a thunderous boom. Perhaps it was the thunder. A woman came to me and cradled me in her arms.

I possess memory blips, from my life as a toddler, of my mother sick and frail wandering through my grandparent's house.

In other cinematic type flashbacks, Uncle Leon, Aunt Linda, Aunt Della and Aunt Virginia are caring me for. They sew my clothing and Aunt Virginia is teaching me to read at age four. The first word that I learned to spell was "war". My mother is not with me during those times. She was in the hospital for long periods of time. My mother would come for me later after she was well. We would move into our shanty.

Chapter Seven

The Return of Pa Daddy

(1960-1961)

About three years later, Pa Daddy returned from whence he had gone. Like an exiled dictator, he returned to our small family farm. I was about two years old when he left and had no concept of who he was. The farm had functioned during his absence under the management of his oldest son, Uncle John. Days before Pa Daddy's arrival, there had been much conversation among my relatives about his impending return. It seemed that some dreaded his return. However, some relatives relished his return because of disagreements among themselves during his absence. Some boasted that it was going to be different when Pa Daddy returned.

I remembered walking up the road from my mother's shanty into my grandparents' farmyard. A broad shouldered and stocky man with close cropped salt and pepper hair was standing at the edge of the farmyard. He was wearing bibbed dungarees, a long sleeved shirt, brogans, and a wide brim straw hat that was worn evenly on the crown of his head. The man was in his fifties and nearly six feet tall. He had light brownish skin and was well shaven with a well-trimmed handlebar mustache. He resembled an oriental wrestler. The man, who was undoubtedly Pa Daddy, was scrutinizing the activities that were occurring in the farmyard. He supervised the activities without uttering a word and his face was expressionless. He stood stone like and only his narrowed eyes moved.

I saw my uncles, aunts and older cousins employed in a variety of tasks. Uncle John, who wore a cap rakishly on his head, and Uncle Leon were cutting lengths of wood on a large table saw, while others were cleaning and repairing farming implements.

Other of my relatives were weeding gardens and harvesting the vegetable crops. Some were feeding chickens, pigs, goats and other livestock. Someone had led the mule from its stable and was cleaning it. I saw no idle hands and everyone was animated and moving swiftly. It seemed like an invisible whip was being cracked over their heads.

Cousin Howard seemed pleased that Pa Daddy was back and at the helm of the operation, because Howard smiled broadly as he worked. Uncle John sternly rebuked him for his jovial behavior and Cousin Howard's smile changed to a frown. Cousin Howard then grumbled some undetectable words under his breath. Pa Daddy was not impressed by the trivial argument and continued to watch the relatives, who were working, like an eagle watching a field of jumping rabbits. His face remained expressionless. Pa Daddy had returned and despite his absence, none dared to oppose him.

Since I was five years old, and had not grown up under Pa Daddy's strict scrutiny as his children and my older cousins, I had no reasons to be apprehensive of him. I have often heard it said that Pa Daddy was a mean man, but I never saw him that way.

I learned from conversations with my uncle and aunts that Pa Daddy assigned them various chores to accomplish. If they failed to complete the chore, they were beaten. Therefore, they had to do what Pa Daddy told them or suffer corporal punishment.

After his return, I was assigned to walk behind the wooden tobacco sled that was drawn by the mule through the rows of the tobacco field. As my older relatives cropped tobacco and threw it into the wooden sled, some of it would fall out.

Cropping tobacco involved pulling about three leaves or more off the tobacco stalk. Since tobacco ripens from the bottom of the stalk and then upwards, the bottom leaves are pulled off or cropped first. The greener upper leaves are left in place until they ripened or turned a yellowish or brownish color. Therefore, people harvesting tobacco have to return about every several days during the harvesting season to remove the next three or so leaves that would have ripened. It could take five visits or more to the same tobacco stalks over a two to three month period to remove all of the tobacco from the stalks. The longer the tobacco stayed on the stalk the stronger the cigarette. The last leaves to be harvested from the stalk were at the top. These leaves are used to make cigars. The tobacco stalks were typically over five feet in height.

The sides of the tobacco sled consisted of a wooden frame covered with ripped open burlap livestock feed sacks. The sled did not have wheels and had wooden runners like a bobsled on the bottom. A sled with wheels on it would have bogged down in the mud between the rows of tobacco plants. I picked up discarded tobacco leaves from the ground and threw them back into the sled. No harvested tobacco leaves were left to rot in the field.

At the end of the day's work, Pa Daddy would be seated in the farmyard at a table. He would count money and pile it in stacks. He would give token money allowances to those who helped harvest the tobacco. Pa Daddy would also give portions of meat to his adult children who lived in their own shanties near the farm if they participated in the slaughter of livestock during killing season or the late fall.

Aunt Linda persuaded me to approach Pa Daddy and stand at a distance from him. I stood there for a short time and then he smiled broadly and beckoned me to him. I moved shyly towards him and Pa Daddy gave me a dollar for my day's work. As a five-year old, I considered a dollar as wealth. During the late nineteen fifties a dollar would buy a soda pop for five cents and two to three large cookies for one penny.

At times, I would wander through my grandparent's house and Pa Daddy would be engaged in conversations with his children and other relatives. I heard him mention on occasions that he regretted that a tragedy happened at the farm and that it was an accident. Pa Daddy on those few occasions would smile at me with compassion, but I did not know what the tragic accident encompassed.

Years later, when I was older, the full ramifications of my dream about thunder were explained to me. It is a secret that still haunts the small farm and those persons, who were reared there, and imposes liabilities throughout the generations. It is a secret that is rarely whispered about but it caused anguish over the course of time for those who inhabited the farm.

It seemed that a cloud hung over the farm after the tragic accident years before. Needless to say, the accident caused repercussions throughout my family. Undoubtedly, it had a negative effect on the persons that were present that tragic night and became a burden that affected future generations of my family.

Inevitably, the innocent and even those who are born in the future inherit the burdens of the mistakes and wrongs committed by their predecessors. The burdens are eased as the generations that lived during those bad times pass on into eternity and eventually, memories of the tragic event fade away.

Chapter Eight

The Repercussions

(1960-1968)

The secret seemed to have its consequences, because a short time after Pa Daddy's return, most of his children, who were adults, began their exodus from the farm. Most of his adult children and grandchildren were physically tempered by the daily rigors of farm work. Like persons who had been stranded too long in the desert without water, his children and grandchildren were discovering oasis in the cities.

However the cloud of secrecy that hung over them at the farm followed them to the city. Like invading Huns, my relatives would change the course of events at the cities. Uncle Leon arrived in Virginia during the nineteen sixties, where he met Aunt Shirley and later married her. Uncle John traveled to the Raleigh-Durham area of North Carolina and settled with his small family there.

My father came to the farm during nineteen sixty-one, when most of my relatives were leaving the confines of the farm. He took my mother, brother, sister and I away from our shanty that had been home for two years. We moved into a house in the nearby city. My brother and I were powerful brutes, tempered by farm work and the romp and tumble-wrestling matches with our older cousins. Our country slang and our strange manners informed our adolescent peers that we were country folk. Thus came challenges from our peers. After grueling wrestling bouts and opponents fallen by our efficient boxing skills, courtesy of Uncle Leon, my younger brother George and I gained respect.

When I entered the first grade at elementary school in the city I learned about fear and intimidation. It is important to address these issues at this point because it seemed that Pa Daddy used these methods in the rearing of his children and in the operation of the family farm.

I was to discover the meaning of fear from my first grade teacher, Mrs. Devaughn. When my father brought me to school on the first day, surprisingly he knew the teacher, as she was a distant cousin of his. This all seemed to my advantage, but I discovered quickly that it had no bearing on the draconian way that Mrs. Devaughn maintained discipline in her class.

During 1961, when I first attended school, corporal punishment was permitted and meted out frequently for any infractions of the rules. I found that Mrs. Devaughn was a strict disciplinarian but a skillful teacher also. Since she had over thirty students to tutor, she maintained strict order by brutally administering spankings with a huge paddle. She would also walk up and down the rows of pupils at the classroom and stand over students with a huge black pencil in her hand or a ruler. Daydream and fiddling around resulted in Mrs. Devaughn asking the student to place his or her hands on their desk palms down. She would then rap the student's fingers several times with a pencil or ruler. The raps to the fingers always brought tears. It seemed that since she did not want to waste time disciplining students, Mrs. Devaughn would make a lasting example out of a few students for even the slightest violations. One male student was forced to bend over double for a half-hour with his fingers touching his toes. He was placed on display in front of his classmates. Mrs. Devaughn administered swats to the male student's buttocks with a paddle while he was bent over. The sounds emitted by the swats of the paddle were loud. He was required to remain in that position after the swats were delivered. Mrs. Devaughn would then talk about a subject matter and within minutes revisit the student, who was bent over, and spank his buttocks some more. She would do this several times over the half-hour period. Undoubtedly, we other students would cringe. For months after the brutal punishment, we students followed the rules to the letter.

Since I was the biggest and strongest student, Mrs. Devaughn devised another demoralizing punishment for me. I was caught daydreaming. I was reminiscing about being at the farm and playing in the stream with my toy boats. Mrs. Devaughn announced that I would be locked in the classroom after she and the other students departed, as my punishment. I imagined that she was not serious. However, when she cautioned me at the end of the school day not to leave and locked the door of the classroom behind her, I had a problem. She told me upon her departure that she would let me out the next morning. After her departure, I became frantic and screamed and yelled. Within minutes a janitor came, unlocked the door and let me out of the classroom. I ran past him terrified and kept running the entire two miles to my house.

Of course, Mrs. Devaughn was a rare breed of teacher but there were a couple of other teachers that I encountered over the years who showed no compassion when meting out corporal punishment.

I know that with the nine children that Pa Daddy reared, draconian punishments similar to those meted out by Mrs. Devaughn were used. Granted, the methods maintain an orderly coexistence among families, but it undoubtedly left some mental scars on the receivers of the punishments. I can relate to the fact that there were economic hard times back during the past, which could have influenced the way, children were raised. However, as parents became better educated in more modern schools and people had more access to the media, most draconian methods of punishments were eventually abolished. Parenting skills are now better than those of the early years.

I have attempted to explain how a relationship of love and apprehension existed between Pa Daddy and his children. Inevitably, some of his children would have mixed emotions about him during their later lives.

Some years later when Pa Daddy was over seventy years old, he would explain his actions to some of his children, who came to visit him after his departure from the farm. It seemed that his explanations about his actions were apologetic but he justified the necessity of his actions also.

Sometimes, people have to put the past behind them and move on. Granted, some of life experiences while growing up are not beds of roses, but people have to reflect more on the positive interactions of their parent and child relationships.

Mrs. Devaughn's draconian methods seemed cruel but her teaching methods were efficient. Therefore, I gained a wealth of knowledge from her. Today, if Mrs. Devaughn were still alive, I would invite her as a guest to my house. Sometimes, life is about taking the good with the bad, thinking positive and moving ahead to bigger and better things.

Life in the city was adventurous but my mother was often hospitalized. Therefore, my sister, brother and I learned quickly how to wash dishes, clean house and do a variety of other chores. By age eight, I was cooking small evening meals to relieve the burden on my father, who worked each day as a stevedore unloading ships at a port near Wilmington, North Carolina.

My father lifted and unloaded bagged commodities, as a stevedore, that weighed well over two hundred pounds and dwarfed him. My father weighed one hundred and sixty pounds and was just over five feet six inches tall. Needless to say, he was a small powerhouse of a man. Uncle Leon, Aunt Virginia and Aunt Linda, who were teenagers, often came from the confines of the farm, where they lived with Pa Daddy and Granny. They would bring gifts for my siblings and I during their visits. Granny would also come and visit us on occasions.

My mother would come from the hospital and stay home for long periods of time and then she would return to the hospital. During times when mother was not in the hospital, father would drive mother and us siblings to the farm to visit my grandparents. My father would not drive up to the farm if he saw Pa Daddy's truck there. He would stop at the entrance to the farm and we would walk about half a block up the dirt road to the main house. My father would then drive back to town alone and pick us up later.

If my grandfather's truck were not parked at the farm, my father would drive up to the house and park his car with the front of it facing the road. Later, when I grew older, the significance of why father never visited with Pa Daddy would be explained. However, there seemed to be an unwavering friendship between my father and the remainder of my relatives.

A new barn stood at the rear of the house during the sixties, because my adolescent cousins and I had destroyed the older one by fire during the late fifties. My description of the destruction of the previous barn is an understatement. I will not elaborate however, on the circumstances of the barn's destruction.

There were some sad days at our home in the city. On those days, of which there were few, my father would grow sad and exclaim, "I do not know why he pointed it (shotgun) at my mother." Then there were times that father would get angry and say the same thing.

When I was thirteen or fourteen years old, my father and mother explained the death of my paternal grandmother to me. I was shocked and hurriedly searched my parent's faces with my eyes to digest what they had just told me. The serious expressions on their faces communicated to me that they were telling me the truth about the incident. Then, the strange comments that my father had made during my younger years about pointing "it" at his mother made sense. "It" was his reference to my maternal grandfather's shotgun. My parents' comments also explained why I never saw my maternal grandfather and father meet with each other during my lifetime. It seemed that a burden of sadness crept upon me the day that my parents revealed the awful secret to me. This burden has been with me ever since, but I never blamed anyone for what happened that awful night. I was old enough at age thirteen to adequately judge the character of my fellow family members. I had seen no one in my family, whom I would categorize as a murderer

There were times during the nineteen sixties, when we as a family, would sit at the dinner table and swap small talk. Father, mother and us siblings would each recount a humorous event that we were involved in. On those days, my father would be very happy. My mother, who sometimes suffered from the effects of her illness, would recount stories about events from the past. We would notice that mother would slightly modify the story, because it would be her one-hundredth telling of the same story. However, mother would be very close to accuracy during her retelling of stories. Sometimes, my father would assist mother and point out some minor discrepancies in her recollections. My mother would then laugh loudly and tell my father that he was mistaken and not her. Then my father and mother would playfully shove at each other and humorously argue about who recounted the correct version of a particular event. This is how I came to learn about my family's past.

On occasions my father's flamboyant cousin, Dudley, would drive my brother, George, and I to his pig farm in the county. There was a striking resemblance between Cousin Dudley and my father. My father was also flamboyant like Cousin Dudley, but Cousin Dudley was a bit more adept at it.

Cousin Dudley drove a pickup truck, which he kept stocked with Mountain Dew ™ soft drinks. He always drove his truck at lightning speeds and avoided traffic jams by driving on the grassy shoulders of the roadways at fast speeds and past the stalled traffic. He would drive his truck with one hand and drink Mountain Dew with the other hand. Cousin Dudley would give my brother and I his soft drink of preference to drink also.

Cousin Dudley owned a house at his pig farm and his first cousin, a rotund man named "Lin", resided with him. Cousin Lin was a master at preparing southern cuisine. I must have inherited genes similar to his, because I am skillful in a kitchen also. However, Cousin Lin was a predictable cook. During our trips to their house, Cousin Lin would always be cooking beans each time we visited, but beans of different varieties. He would put various cuts of pork meat in the beans for seasoning. Cousin Lin cooked Pinto Beans with hog jaw.

On another visit, he would be cooking Lima Beans with ham hocks. On our next visit, he would be cooking Navy Beans with smoked pig feet.

Upon our return weeks later, Cousin Lin would be cooking Field Peas with smoked streak of lean fatback. During the five-year period that we visited my father's first cousins, the menu was always beans of various types with various cuts of smoked pork.

I think at some point, that even Cousin Dudley grew tired of eating beans from Cousin Lin's scores of bean recipes. However, beans and rice with a bit of pork for seasoning was an inexpensive recipe and provided substance during grueling days of farm work.

Cousin Lin had a vision problem and a sleeping disorder. He would always give my brother, sister, and I, a few coins of money during our visits. He would hold up a quarter closely to his glasses and conclude that it was a dime. He would then give us a quarter each. My siblings and I would burst our sides laughing at Cousin Lin's antics. I always suspected that he feigned not being able to see the coins, as a game that he played with us.

On other occasions, Cousin Lin would ride me in his car and at stoplights I would hear him snoring. He would be fast asleep but miraculously, when the light changed to green, he would wake up and continue driving. Cousin Lin was a fastidious eater. He chuckled one day and recounted how the floorboards of the house broke under his weight and he fell through.

I will always remember Cousin Lin and Cousin Dudley as being very hospitable and kind. May they rest in peace.

On a two occasions, my father took my siblings and me to a

house that he owned in an adjacent county. We would take furniture from the tall rambling house that he inherited from his mother. This is where my father and his mother lived for many years and this is also where I lived for a couple of years after my birth during the nineteen fifties.

My mother moved into the house after marrying my father, therefore she resided in her mother-in-law's house. My mother pushed me in a baby carriage through the fields surrounding my paternal grandmother's house and harvested some of the crops. My sister, Helen, who was two years older than I, would trudge behind my mother as she pushed me in the carriage.

I would often comment to my father during visits to his house, that it was a beautiful house and larger than the one that we rented in at the city. I yearned to move from the city into the house. My father would look at me with a slight smile on his face, when I mentioned us moving back into the grandiose house. He would sigh and comment that he did not know if we would ever move back there. I would then see him looking around at the furnishings in the house. It seemed that he was silently reliving the good times that he had cherished at the house. Father never took us children to his mother's grave.

Over the years, the grandiose house, without paint and proper care, deteriorated and collapsed. Only the bricks of the statuesque chimney remained. I realize now that the house brought back too many memories for my father. In the end, the house was swept away like the sands of time, and now it exists only as a memory in my mind of what could have been.

For me, not being able to live in the house and experience it has left a blank spot in my life. It is like watching a movie and you are led up to an interesting part and the film breaks. The film is damaged in one large section and now you can not see the segment of the movie that the dialogue was leading up to. Then you are forced to imagine what happened in that segment of the story. In my situation, I have to imagine how life would have been while living in the house with my parents and my paternal grandmother.

But then, there is also the flip side of the situation. What if the tragedy had never happened? I can only surmise that my life would have been different today, but would I have been better situated. Sometimes, I feel that my life's situations resulted in me being at specific places at specific times.

Undoubtedly, my interplay with other people has had both positive and negative impacts on their lives. The people that I had a negative impact on were incarcerated for committing crimes. In retrospect, the criminals' victims gained from the criminals' downfalls.

I look at my children, who were raised in to fine adults. Obviously, I was where I needed to be.

In my opinion a series of events, one tragic, brought me to where I am now. This is my perspective on life, but then after evaluating my own arguments, I would have traded this life for a life with my paternal grandmother. Her life was more important than anything that I could have possibly achieved. I will not say yet that the life that I have now is a reward, because over the course of time, my destiny will become known.

My Father kept a picture of his mother in our living room and his bedroom. She was a very beautiful woman and it would have been an honor for me to have known her.

Relative to people who owned land in rural areas during the nineteen fifties, my paternal grandmother's gravesite is in a wooded area in a county of North Carolina. I have often wondered why some people do not visit the graves of their deceased relatives. It seems sometimes that the affection was so strong, that visits are soul rendering. Especially, if the death was a tragedy.

I honor my father today for his compassion and understanding and for keeping his family together after he suffered a personal loss. Some day soon, I will go and find my paternal grandmother's grave. I will weep and then heal my wounds.

Chapter Nine

The Trials and Tribulations of Pa Daddy

(1967-1995)

During the nineteen sixties, and perhaps sometime during 1967 or 1968, Pa Daddy departed the farm and began what seemed to be a self-imposed exile. Perhaps a dictatorship can be wrought with problems if you do not have a strong coalition of support or a means of cheap labor.

But then, perhaps Pa Daddy felt that he had done all that he could do to rear nine children. The tragedy at the farm had changed things to some extent and even someone, as mentally tough as Pa Daddy, had lost some of the motivation that he was reputed for. Life is this way sometimes. A person pursues a goal and while accomplishing it, a tragedy or some other significant pitfall occurs. Then one ponders the negative things that occurred and decides that it is not worthwhile to continue. The person realistically looks down the road and imagines how things are going to be in the future. If the picture is bleak, then perhaps its time to move on down the highway.

It seemed that like a professional boxer, who had reigned as champion for too long, Pa Daddy threw in the towel and departed. He turned over the operation of the farm to Granny. Pa Daddy would return on occasions to visit Granny. Some of his children criticized Pa Daddy for leaving the family farm, but it seemed that it was not done openly. It seemed that he had a sudden desire for travel and adventure. His desires resulted in him meeting a woman, who later became his companion, however he and Granny never divorced.

Some years after Pa Daddy departed the family farm, I visited him at his home on the outskirts of the city. I was about fourteen years old and a big strapping youth. Pa Daddy paid me to do odd jobs for him around his house and this included tending to his flock of chickens.

One day he instructed me to kill a chicken and prepare it for consumption. Though I was raised on the farm, until I departed at the age of six for the city, where I lived with my parents and siblings, I had never killed a chicken.

I had seen Granny skillfully grasp a chicken by the head and neck with one hand and with a twist of her wrist snap the chicken's neck. Granny's technique was swift and painless. I never developed Granny's technique; therefore I hovered, with a hatchet in my hand, over the chicken. I extended the chicken's neck by pulling its head from its body. As I paused to deliver the fatal blow, I could not find the determination to do it. I released the chicken and waited for Pa Daddy to return home.

When Pa Daddy arrived home an hour later, he pulled a huge bag of money from behind his truck seat and asked if I had completed the chores. Pa Daddy looked at me kindly. I confessed that everything was accomplished except the killing of the chicken. I looked rather comical standing there, a strapping youth that could not kill a chicken. Pa Daddy's face filled with mirth and he laughed. My face changed many shades of red. He then paid me for the chores and gave me a five-pound box of smoked sausages to take home to my mother. I thanked him and rushed off for home.

However, there were more sad times when Aunt Margaret, who was Uncle Leon's older sister, passed away during the early nineteen seventies from a heart related illness. I was about sixteen years old and sitting in Aunt Margaret's apartment prior to the time of her funeral services.

Suddenly, a stern looking woman dressed in stylish dark clothes walked into the apartment among the waiting mourners and sat down. There were incredulous looks on my relatives' faces and

Granny began to shriek disparaging comments at the woman. Uncle John, who towered over the woman, limped towards her and asked, "Woman, why you come here? You got no right. You got no respect."

Seconds later, I heard Uncle John yelling for assistance, and he was wrestling with the woman despite his physical disabilities. I looked incredulously at Uncle John and wondered if he had gone mad. Uncle John then yelled that the woman had a gun. Suddenly, I spied a gun in the woman's hand and Uncle John with a strong grip on her wrist. It seemed that things began to move in slow motion. I leaped into the fray and wrestled a thirty- eight-caliber pistol from the woman's hand.

Then incredulously, I saw several round tinfoil covered objects fall out of the woman's pocketbook and strike the floor. I gazed at the woman and her eyes locked onto mine. She had a mean expression on her face. Suddenly, the woman's eyes startled me. Her eyes looked like those of a snake and they seemed to have no soul. I was forced to pause as she fixed her gaze on me.

It seemed symbolic of the Greek mythological monster, *Medusa*. Medusa was a creature who had a hideous face with withering snakes attached to her head. According to Greek mythology, Medusa's stare could turn men to stone. I moved from the woman and Uncle John grabbed the gun from me and waited for the arrival of a police officer.

Pa Daddy arrived at the apartment in time to see his companion handcuffed and led away by the police. Pa Daddy appeared undaunted by the incident and displayed a composed and expressionless demeanor. He waited at the apartment for the family car to take mourners to the funeral.

Several of my cousins examined the tinfoil packets that the woman had dropped. They were various coins of money sprinkled with a white powdery substance and wrapped with tinfoil. Granny shuddered upon seeing the coins and warned my cousins not to pick them up with their hands and to dispose of them in a Dumpster.

Years later, during my college studies, I learned that coins of money (coinage) are used in the practices of witchcraft. Sometimes the coins are doused with powder and other substances to supposedly create a magical spell. Sometimes money and other items, which I will not divulge, are placed in pouches and worn around the neck to ward off evil spells or to protect the wearer from harm. Therefore, the coins that fell out of Pa Daddy's girlfriend's pocket book were talismans or objects supposedly having magical powers

Later, we were travelling in the funeral possession motorcade towards the family cemetery in the county, when a limousine ahead of us pulled onto the shoulder of the roadway. The hearse that was in front of the limousine had pulled over also and it was having mechanical problems. Within seconds or minutes, a hand extended itself from the limousine's window and one of my cousins dropped several tinfoil-covered coins from her hand onto the ground. Mysteriously, the hearse cranked up and the motorcade continued to the gravesite.

Granny was informed of the incident with the hearse stalling and that a cousin had kept some of the coins. There was much consternation on Granny's face after this revelation and she stated that no good would come of it. My other older women relatives then whispered among themselves and then walked off with their heads bowed.

The three goddess of fate wove the threads of life, but then they paused. It seemed that this day would be of significance to things to come.

I recalled that Pa Daddy returned home in a sense. During 1994, he departed his life and joined his ancestors before him in eternity. He died at a nursing home where he had resided for more than a year, after his woman companion stopped caring for him. I wept. His companion, the woman with the snake eyes, discarded Pa

Daddy like he was rubbish and swore that he was penniless. She was not seen at his funeral.

Granny removed Pa Daddy's insurance policy from her storage trunk and notified other relatives of Pa Daddy's demise. Granny had maintained an insurance policy on Pa Daddy. Cousin Earl, who had several friends in the funeral business, made funeral arrangements. This was the last funeral that Cousin Earl arranged, because just over a year later, Cousin Earl passed into eternity also. Uncle John did not attend Pa Daddy's funeral. Though they cooperated together in operating the farm, there was a divide between them.

Old wounds continue to fester, even now after Pa Daddy's death. Pa Daddy became a deacon at a church before his death and eased his burdens before departing into eternity. Pa Daddy confessed his sins before his death, sincerely regretted some things he did and prayed for forgiveness. I give accolades to Granny because she has never said harsh things against him in my presence.

I will honor Pa Daddy forever because he did change and I witnessed it. Pa Daddy's legacy as a stern but fair man lives on. In the end, we, his blood kin, carried him to his final resting-place.

I learned a lesson from the death of Pa Daddy. Sometimes a man strays away from home to be with a woman, who cherishes him only for his possessions. When the man departs this life, the woman has no more use for him. Then a woman with true devotion for him brings him home for burial. Perhaps, he should have never departed from where he was. It was ironic that with all of the power that Pa Daddy possessed at the farm that his weakness was his desire for a wicked woman. It was symbolic in some ways to the love story of Samson and Delilah, because the woman betrayed Pa Daddy in the end.

Chapter Ten

The Intricacies of Fate and Destiny

(1962-2000)

When Uncle Leon was in his early adult years and dating, I would see him departing Granny's house, where he lived, well dressed. Uncle Leon had a fancy gold colored watch that he had paid over one hundred dollars for and he would flash the watch on his wrist and boast of its expense. It seemed that only a short time after Uncle Leon purchased the watch that he stood on Granny's porch and looked at it with distaste. The watch had ceased functioning. Uncle Leon ripped the watch off his wrist, commented that it was a piece of crap, and threw it into the woods. Uncle Leon then made it a point later to tell his siblings and other relatives to never buy that particular brand of watch. Uncle Leon was often spontaneous and did things sometimes on the spur of the moment with no regrets later. It seemed that Uncle Leon could always convince himself through conversations with others that though it might have been thoughtless to do certain things, that the circumstances warranted it. Uncle Leon was a very intelligent man and made sound decisions, albeit he made some brash ones also.

Uncle Leon was assistant manager at a fast food restaurant in Wilmington, North Carolina. Years later, I worked as assistant manager the same restaurant. Uncle Leon and I both worked as security officers but during different times and places. He joined the military and was medically retired. I joined the military and retired after twenty years of service. There are many similarities in the occupations that we held. Uncle Leon had a burning desire to become a police officer. I was in the United States Army Military Police Corps and employed as a civilian police officer after my military career. So many things that he did, I did also.

After Uncle Leon's death, Aunt Shirley told me that she was happy that Uncle Leon spent the previous weekend with her before the tragic accident. She also told me that Uncle Leon had always wanted to visit Disney World and take the family. Uncle Leon and his family went to Disney World about one year prior to his death. From Aunt Shirley's accounts, it seemed that Uncle Leon enjoyed Disney world more than his adult children and grandson did. Aunt Shirley told me that she was appalled at Uncle Leon's behavior at Disney World. He threw balloons full of water on people at an event. It seemed that Uncle Leon wanted to make the event more exciting. Uncle Leon was spontaneous as always.

Uncle Leon had tried to contact me the weekend before his death so that I could visit with him. It happened that my brother, George, had come to Virginia that weekend during some of his aimless travels. I was forced to drive him back to North Carolina that weekend. Therefore, I missed meeting Uncle Leon the weekend prior to his tragic death. Sometimes, I wonder what significance that weekend would have had on the days that followed.

I have heard many people talk about fate and remember the origination of the word "fate" from Greek Mythology. According to Greek Mythology there were three goddesses who were fate. The goddesses were called weavers. Clotho, the Spinner, spun the thread of life or what is called a person's existence. Lachesis, she was the goddess who decided how long a person would live and assigned a destiny to each person. Atropos was the carrier of the shears and cut the person's thread of life at an appointed time. (Encarta, 1997-2000)

Many people say that people died because it was their time to die or it was their fate. Of course, there are people who believe that someone or a whole family can be cursed and that the family's demise was as foreseeable as the changing of the seasons.

In my opinion, some people die unnecessarily and a review of the chain of events that occurred before their death indicated careless acts on their parts.

I personally have shook hands with the Grim Reaper on several occasions. I have survived some extraordinary automobile wrecks.

During August 2000, I was at work and began to feel ill. I placed my hand on my chest and my heart was racing. I then attempted to call my family doctor but a recording said that she was at a meeting. My condition continued to worsen.

Like in a dream, I could now hear ancient West African drums beating with a rhythmic sound. The drums are sending a message that someone is seriously ill. A witch doctor is needed.

My ancestors, who had passed before me, assembled and waited. The three goddesses of fate paused in their weaving. I could hear the voices of my ancestors. Some were saying, "He should have taken better care of his health." Others were saying, "He sure looks bad." "He drinks too much of that Light Beer." "His schedule is just too hectic." "I hope it ain't too late." One or two other voices said, "I think he going to make it, because the rescue squad is coming."

The three goddesses of fate looked on. Atropos picked up her shears and then checked her scroll. It was not my time yet, because she put the shears away. Then I am reminded of the earlier follies of my life. It seemed that I was sitting in a movie theater alone.

The first movie was titled, "1959". There I was a small boy, fishing with Aunt Della in the pond beneath the railroad crossing. I had grown impatient with fishing and jumped in the water to grab a fish. I began to drown and my lungs filled with water. I surfaced and blew water out of my nose and mouth. Aunt Della grabbed me and dragged me ashore. Aunt Della is elated. *This time she was not helpless, and she was able to save a life.*

The second movie was titled "1967". I stripped off my clothes and jumped into a lake before my other friends. I could not swim and began to drown. On the third occasion that I bobbed to the surface of the lake, my brother and some friends rescued me.

There is a scene from 1971, where I am driving a Volkswagen with faulty brakes and collide with a car in an intersection. I am thrown out of the driver's window of the Volkswagen and land on my back thirty feet from my car in a traffic lane. Cars screech to a halt and avoid hitting me. I am rushed to the hospital by ambulance.

The next movie is titled, " 1976". I am driving a Military Police Jeep and following the German Police to a traffic accident scene where an U.S. military vehicle is involved. The jeep is unable to negotiate a sharp curve in the road ahead and it is now riding on the edges of the two tires on the passenger side. I let the steering wheel go and the driver's side of the jeep slams back down onto the pavement. I continue to drive to the accident scene.

A movie titled 1990 is displayed on the screen. I am sitting in a traffic jam on the autobahn near Wiesbaden, Germany. I am in the rear seat of a military van. There is a sudden screeching of tires. My head turns and a large car rams the rear of the van. The van is totally demolished. An airforce doctor at a nearby airforce hospital is examining me. He says, "That big muscular chest of yours saved you, after the bench seat with the two soldiers on it broke loose from the van's floor and hit you in the chest. You suffered a bruised heart but it will mend. A man in less physical condition than you would have not survived."

I am shown several other movies about my close brushes with death, which includes another scene with me riding in a jeep, which almost rolls over during 1986, while I am stationed in Korea. Sergeant Kim, a South Korean soldier, who is augmented to the same Military Police Company as I, is driving me to an incident where a soldier is threatening to jump off a building. Sergeant Kim is attempting to negotiate a curve in the road ahead at a high speed and I caution him to slow down. However, we are at the edge of the curve and both wheels on Sergeant Kim's side of the jeep come up off the pavement and I am dangling out the front passenger side of the jeep, where it is riding on the two passenger tires. I only barely stay inside of the jeep by bracing myself against a safety strap that extends across the jeep's passenger side. The jeep has a vinyl top but no sides. Miraculously, the tires on Sergeant Kim's side of the jeep slam back down onto the pavement. My relief is cut short as the jeep instantly spins into reverse and leaves the roadway. It travels backwards down a steep hill and towards a newly planted rice field. It is during the early summer and the rice field is filled with water that is knee deep, rice plants, and smelly human excrement that Koreans use as fertilizer. I glance backwards briefly, shake my head and muse, "Well, out of the frying pan and now into a field of crap." It was going to be hard to live down this particular excursion. Then, miraculously the rear of our jeep slams into a tree and we are saved from a smelly bath. I jump out of the jeep onto the bank of the hill. I notice that the tree that stopped the jeep is the only tree at the bottom of the lengthy hill for a mile in either direction. How lucky can you get?

I am brought back to reality when I am placed in an ambulance and taken to a local hospital for treatment.

People would call my survival of several near fatal accidents or incidents as miraculous. Does it mean that I am also marked by a curse that is decimating my family? I would care not to think so, but I am well insured. The odds don't seem to be in my favor.

I have survived some near fatal accidents because of my ability to keep situations under control. I found that another important key to survival is not pushing yourself beyond your limitations. Without a doubt, rest or sleep makes for an alert human who can cheat the Grim Reaper when things start spinning out of control. But then sometimes, there is no way out of some critical situations and the results are death and injury.

I recall an old adage that supposedly originated from the Japanese Samurai. It says that to fear death is to die many times before you actually do. I also like the Japanese adage about living each day like it going to be your last. That makes a lot of sense to me, therefore I thrive to live each day like it is my last.

Sometimes, I envy some inmates on death row because they know the exact date of they demise. Some death row inmates know the precise hour and minute of their death, therefore death is something they can plan for. But what appalls me are those damn appeals and the condemned getting a stay of execution at the last possible hour. Personally, I would say, "The hell with that." That is too much anxiety. If I committed the crime, I would not want any delays on my one way ticket to hell. That's my feeling on it, because I like doing things on schedule and do not like delays.

It seems that a dark cloud hangs over me. While I was in law enforcement, there never was a dull moment and life threatening situations abound. I sighed with relief when assigned as a desk sergeant at a large military base. However, like a dark cloud, there was total mayhem while I was on duty. Record numbers of homicides, assaults, rapes, drunk drivers and accidental deaths of many categories occurred and were reported. It became too noticeable when patrolmen ribbed me and said, "It going to be a wild ride tonight with you working." It seemed wise to suspend any activities while I was on the desk.

Fatigued by the ever-going onslaught of incidents, I answered my private phone at home with, "Police Desk. A patrol has been dispatched to your location."

During the times when I was not being worked to death, I dreamed about death. There is nothing wrong with dreams as long as they are pleasant ones. My dreams were premonitions of events that would happen in the future. I did not read the newspaper about several plane crashes that occurred. I knew the details from my dreams. Most of the dreams were very vivid and it seemed I was present when the events occurred. I could feel the intensity of the events.

One night, I had a dream about a boxing team perishing in a plane crash in Europe. It was an intense dream. In the dream, I spied a water tower near the crash site and it had a banner displayed on it. The banner had the identity of the boxing team on it. I woke up and exclaimed, "Come on now. Give me a break." It seemed that my dream was a comedy. I told a close confidant about this dream. Well, the dream came true but because the plane was overbooked, only one member of the team perished. Over a dozen boxers were spared due to overbooking.

I have often heard it said that if man could travel back in time, that he could change certain past events. However, there could be a paradox, because it could change things that shaped the future, where, the time traveler came from. I often look at my dreams from the same perspective.

I have dreams only rarely now because of a sleeping disorder. The disorder does not allow me to get REM sleep or "rapid eye movement" sleep. REM sleep is essential for entering into a dream state. Of course, there are ways to correct my sleeping disorder or sleep apnea. The pitfall is that if I correct the disorder, I will start having strange dreams again.

An issue at this point is whether Uncle Leon had psychic abilities or was he just lucky at guessing things about my sister in law. I will only comment that it could be a family thing.

Earlier, I described the tragedy that occurred at my grandparent's farm. It was ironic that by my father and grandmother going to a practitioner of the black arts in an attempt to save my mother's life, that my paternal grandmother was accidentally killed.

Since my mother was severely ill when Pa Daddy saw her at the hospital, it would have been reasonable to assume that her illness from the birth of my brother weeks earlier had been ongoing.

The issue is why my father and his mother did not take my mother to the hospital earlier to prevent the degree of the infection that she was suffering from. There were probably several reasons for them not taking her to the hospital in a timely fashion.

Over time and after his mother's death, I discovered that my father was very stingy with money in regards to maintaining one's personal health. Also, my father only purchased a few items of clothing for us family members, but we ate fairly well.

However, he supervised grocery shopping and insured that the same amount of money was spent each week for our family of five. During the early 1960s, my father spent $5.00 per week for groceries but then laborers brought home $60.00 to $70.00 a week. A whole chicken for frying cost eighteen cents. Some can goods could be purchased for ten cents a can. My father spent $5.00 for grocery each week and no more than that. He accomplished this by purchasing items for the main evening meal and breakfast meals to cover a seven- day period.

Notice that there were no provisions for lunch meals. When school was in session, my siblings and I received five cents each for the daily lunch meal. During the summer months, we drank lots of water and foraged for figs, cherries, black berries, and other fruits that grew near our neighborhood. My father utilized my brother and I as grocery carriers. He would dispatch us to the various aisles of the grocery store with instructions to bring back specific items. My father never used a grocery list because he bought the same kind of items each week and the same number of items at the same price.

When there was enough food in the cart for seven days, breakfast and supper, he would cease shopping. However, he would occasionally buy desserts for the Sunday meal.

Father would scrutinize the lady operating the cash register and ringing up the groceries. If he saw her enter the wrong price for a product, he would tell her immediately. If groceries cost $6.00, we would use slips of paper at home and conduct an inventory. Since all foods had price labels on them, we could match them against the grocery receipt. After my brother and I tabulated and checked, I would inform my father that he was over charged exactly $1.00, as he had suspected. My father would always comment, "Well, I knew she overcharged us, because I never deviate that much from my mental grocery list." Then my father would order my brother and I to repack everything. My father would then return it to the grocery store. I would stand at a distance to the rear of my father as he diplomatically brought the matter to the cash register clerk's attention. My father would smile and act very gracious while discussing the incident of overcharging. The clerk would then recheck the items, advise my father that he was correct and graciously refund him $1.00.

Of course back during the early 1960s, $1.00 could buy seven hot dogs with the works at the Chuck Wagon Stand that was adjacent to a main road on the outskirts of Wilmington, North Carolina. My father would buy exactly seven hotdogs and my parents would eat two each and us three siblings would eat one hotdog each. A near by soft drink machine and forty cents produced a soft drink for each of us. The soft drinks cost eight cents each.

My father should have been employed at Fort Knox, Kentucky at the gold storage facility. I say this because he locked up important papers, our Sunday clothes for church, the deep freezer with frozen foods, and the engine compartment of his 1963 shiny black Buick. One could see a small padlock and chain dangling from the front grille of his fancy car.

Every Friday evening was a ritual for my father. It started when he got off at work at about five o'clock in the evening. He would instruct my brother and I either to dust off his shiny black Buick or wash it. He allowed us to use our own discretion as long as the car was free of dust and dirt. On occasions, we would wax it. Father would then eat his supper, take a bath, and dress in a baggy suit with shirt and tie that was the fashion during the 1960s. My father would then select a dark color dress hat with a small bird feather on the side of the hatband.

After he was dressed, he would ceremoniously tell my mother, "Annie, I am going on the town. I will be back later." My father would then crank up his Buick, which resembled a small limousine and drive off for town. He would leave his hat on while driving. I guess the hat made him look taller, because he was only about five feet, six inches tall and slight in build. The huge car made him look even smaller.

Well, at this point I am going to describe how my father's habits were relative to destiny or how things occurred that awful night.

Needless to say, people's unwillingness to spend money when one's health is at stake is well documented. I heard a story years ago that there was a woman who inherited billions of dollars because her family owned oil and fuel refineries. The woman's son grew ill with a leg infection and despite the woman's wealth she refused to spend money for his medical treatment. Unfortunately, her son lost a leg because of her stinginess.

My father was never in a hurry to take anyone to the hospital. He was always money conscious.

At the same time, I have heard stories from my father and other relatives about his mother's tenacity with money. She hoarded money also, but did purchase my father at least two new cars with cash money prior to her tragic death. My father was her only child.

There was also another story about how my paternal grandmother acquired considerable amounts of money. It seemed that an uncle of hers, who was an extensive landowner and entrepreneur, died at a ripe old age. The story goes that my paternal grandmother was the first to arrive at her uncle's house after his death. Supposedly, the uncle kept large sums of cash on hand at home and in a safe. Later, other relatives arriving at the house after my paternal grandmother did find money in the safe but it was not substantial.

Later, my paternal grandmother acquired a rather spacious house and placed French doors and other stylish furnishings in it.

Such is fate or the adage that the early bird gets the worm.

Now, it can be surmised that perhaps my father and his mother were in no hurry to seek medical treatment for my mother. Without doubt, this is what Pa Daddy mulled over that night prior to the tragedy.

The other issue concerned the reports of physical abuse that Pa Daddy argued with Granny about. It could be said that my father and his mother could be pleasant the majority of the time, but on occasions they were be vicious and mean during arguments. My mother often told me stories about how my father and his mother use to have vicious arguments when she lived with them. She was amazed that a mother and son could argue at each other to such extremes.

My father possessed a hot temper and I saw him beat my mother once, when I was about eight years old. He spent two months in jail and never beat my mother again. Of course when I reached the age of twelve, I was five feet, nine inches tall and still growing. I was muscular and weighed about one hundred and fifty-five pounds, therefore I was taller than my father was and weighed more than him. My brother George, who was two years younger than me, was about my size also.

Father had a truck and would move furniture for various people. George and I did all the heavy lifting of refrigerators and stoves. In fact, we lifted ninety-five percent of what was loaded onto my father's truck. My father would supervise and beam with pride, when people remarked about the strength of his two sons.

However, taking into consideration that we were powerful brutes, my father had more positive interactions with our mother during those times.

I recall being taught in my psychology classes about women who dote on their sons and feel that no other women are adequate for their sons. Therefore, son and mother relationships of this nature are too tightly interwoven and the mothers are always challenging the abilities of the wives who marry their sons. I have witnessed this, because I have heard men tell wives in their mothers' presence that the wives cook good but not as well as the husbands' mothers. Of course, I have heard wives say, "Well, why didn't you marry your mother?"

It could be surmised that Pa Daddy felt that, his son-in-law, William, should be held responsible for anything that happened to his daughter. Obviously, Pa Daddy had come to his own conclusions about William and his doting mother.

Therefore, on the night in question, during the early summer of 1957, as Pa Daddy sat on his front porch and stewed, the wheels of destiny were turning faster than usual. Well, a wheel that turns too long on an axle without being greased heats up and breaks the bearings or the axle. Without a doubt, all hell was going to break loose that night.

According to Aunt Virginia, she saw Pa Daddy on the night in question, sitting on front porch in the dark. Pa Daddy had his head and eyes turned in only one direction, and that was down the dirt road, which intersected with the main paved highway. Pa Daddy was looking in the direction that any car would take to drive up to his farm. Pa Daddy was sitting on a chair and sprawled backward against the side of the house with the front legs of his chair raised off the porch. The bulk of Pa Daddy's weight rested on the two rear legs of the chair, which was tilted backwards. There was a foreboding expression on Pa Daddy's face.

It can be surmised now that habits like stinginess and nasty personal dispositions can lead to life's misadventures.

Also, there is the issue of self-preservation. My Aunt Della recounted to me that Pa Daddy was "seeing razors" or was furious upon seeing my mother near death at the hospital. I can only imagine that Pa Daddy's demeanor was obvious to my father and his mother that day at the hospital. Of course, my father had heard that Pa Daddy could be a tough man to reckon with.

My father, William, and his mother, Erdell, knew that Pa Daddy and Granny had visited them on several previous occasions about the reports that my mother was being abused.

I guess my father and his mother did not see the warning signs on that ill-fated day and erred by dropping Aunt Della off at the front of my grandparents' house that night.

Of course, the bonds between mothers and sons are strong. It was a mother's instinct that caused my paternal grandmother to make an attempt to wrestle the shotgun from Pa Daddy, after he told my father to get out of the car. My father, Uncle Jesse and Cousin Lawrence were frozen with fear to their seats and could not move, even during the short period when my grandmother was trying to wrestle the shotgun from Pa Daddy.

However, after the shotgun gun accidentally fired into my paternal grandmother's abdomen, the two men as aforementioned exited the car and ran through the woods near my grandparent's house or down the main road leading to the house in fear of their lives. Uncle Jesse, who had gotten out of the car, when Pa Daddy initially brandished the shotgun, departed also.

Uncle John crawled from underneath the porch where he had been hiding and told Pa Daddy that the men had ran, and pointed out Cousin Lawrence who was running through the woods. Pa Daddy was shocked and did not pursue the fleeing men.

My father and his other men relatives then summoned assistance, but my paternal grandmother had died instantly after the shotgun fired.

I was never able to get clear information about what Pa Daddy intended to do to my father that night. Some of my relatives suspected that Pa Daddy was going to shoot him. Other relatives say that they do not know for sure what Pa Daddy's plans were. I surmised that Pa Daddy did not intend to shoot my father. According to my father, Pa Daddy attempted to strike him with the butt of the shotgun, when he exited the car and ran that night.

I witnessed my father running for exercise during the 1960s when he was in his forties, and he had track star potential. Needless to say, my father broke all existing track records for the long distance run that night.

However, I think he had planned to do something in such a way, that my father would live, but there would be no more reports about my mother being abused. Sometimes, you have to make an example out of some people to encourage them to change. The issue of having respect for a man and his immediate family is also of paramount importance.

But, bringing a gun into the situation was ill advised and meting out punishment while you are mad is ill advised as well. It is always best to cool off and rationally plan a course of action that will not produce casualties. A little fisticuffs behind the barn would have been appropriate, and Pa Daddy had some sturdy daughters who could have delivered a whipping as efficient as some men.

Nowadays, it is best to notify the authorities when abuse occurs. They are better organized to handle incidents of abuse. Never take the law into your own hands despite what might occur during life.

Pa Daddy was tried and convicted of second-degree murder and given a fifteen- year- sentence. He served two to three years of his sentence and was released on good behavior. He made women pocketbooks while in prison and he sent them home to Granny and his older daughters. Granny was always happy to receive the pocketbooks.

It is rather obvious now that a chain of negative events that occurred previously precipitated a tragedy. But then sometimes, it takes a tragedy for some people to come to grips with their personal faults and change them. However, in the case of my father, this was not to be the case.

During a petty argument with a friend during October 1997, my father suffered a head injury. Instead of seeking medical attention, he tended to himself and succumbed from the injury. As usual, my father held onto his money. This incident will be explained further as you read through the next chapters.

Aunt Della, my sister, Helen, and I are the only persons living of the seven persons in my father's car that fateless night. Uncle Jesse died of old age twenty to thirty years ago. Cousin Lawrence died of alcoholism during the nineteen sixties. It seemed that the death of his aunt was traumatic, and his taste for alcoholic beverages increased after witnessing her death.

I believe that stinginess is one of the seven deadly sins and like the other six, they all have precipitated tragedies. Stinginess to me is the same as being greedy, especially when it has a negative impact on other people's lives. Perhaps, some people need to do self- evaluations and change their ways. Because in the end, the reasons for their demise are going to be painfully obvious. They will depart their earthly bounds and join their ancestors before them.

Sometimes, there are no second chances.

Chapter Eleven

In Remembrance of the Trucker

(1994-1997)

Before Uncle Leon's untimely death, he and I drove to North Carolina on three occasions for funerals after the deaths of his father, nephew, and sister. It was during our trip from Virginia to North Carolina for his nephew's or my Cousin Earl's funeral during nineteen ninety-five that he told me that he was going to start training big rig drivers on the road. Uncle Leon commented that he could earn more money that way. Of course, Uncle Leon could always devise ways of making extra money, but I discussed the dangers of training drivers with him. I was very straightforward with Uncle Leon and told him that team driving with another driver seemed rather dangerous to me. I remarked that I could not drive that way, because the other person might fall asleep while I was asleep in the bunk compartment. I then humored him by recounting how I fell asleep on the graveyard shift while driving a patrol car at five miles per hour and jumped a curb. Uncle Leon listened to my comments and remarked that he was not concerned about accidents because he had an adequate life insurance policy. Uncle Leon then commented that he would never live to be an old man and then chuckled at his own remarks. I was flabbergasted by my uncle's comments, because he seemed comfortable with what he had said.

Suddenly, Uncle Leon spied a truck stop along Interstate 95 South and motioned for me to pull in there for a late evening meal. Uncle Leon explained that many truckers ate at this particular truck stop including him. It seemed that everyone at the truck stop knew Uncle Leon and surprisingly they all knew him by name.

One trademark of my family is the way that we walk. We walk

with our toes turned slightly inward and our stout bodies lumbering forward like a sumo wrestler. This is how Uncle Leon walked in and around the truck stop looking at the various wares for sale.

I have always believed that Uncle Leon viewed every job or occupation he held as being symbolic, in that you acquire certain habits relative to your line of work. Without a doubt, he would have been a great actor on the silver screen in a variety of roles. I know that the job with the most symbolism to suit his tastes was that of a truck driver. Uncle Leon loved the big rigs or huge transportation trucks because they symbolized tons of horsepower and the need for a rugged man to take charge of all that horsepower and maneuver the trucks. Therefore, my Uncle had at least two pair of western boots, and billed caps that truckers commonly wear.

I was appalled however by his use of chewing tobacco. I strongly believe that he acquired the habit of using chewing tobacco as part of his persona as a trucker. He often had a mouth full of chewing tobacco on our trips to North Carolina for funerals. In fact, we rarely went to North Carolina together unless it was for the funeral of a close relative. The problem with the chewing tobacco was that he would use a soda bottle as a spittoon and put the container in the drink holder of my wife's minivan. Uncle Leon would also stick paper napkins inside of open cups to keep the wads of spit and chewing tobacco remnants from sloshing around. Needless to say, he placed a cup with paper napkins and chewing tobacco spit in the back seat pocket of my wife's minivan. It stayed there for about a month and my wife found it while cleaning her minivan. Ruth knew that Uncle Leon had left it there. It seemed for a while that Uncle Leon and I would be making any future trips to North Carolina in my gas guzzling four- wheel drive pickup truck.

I had a bad experience with chewing tobacco many years ago and that's why I detest people spitting chewing tobacco into soda cans and placing them near the soda cans that other people are drinking from. Of course, if a person is driving a car and reaches unsuspectingly for the drinking can with the chewing tobacco residue, the end results are not appealing.

Cigarette smokers are also notorious for placing cigarette butts into soda cans that are partially filled with soft drink Smokers inadvertently place the soda cans with cigarette butts beside the soft drink can of unsuspecting persons. My wife is a smoker and on our way to Long Island, New York a few years ago, she placed cigarette butts in a soda can, which was unobserved by me. Subsequently, I spewed a mixture of soft drink and cigarette butts onto the dash and inner windshield of our minivan.

Uncle Leon continued to ramble around the wares at the truck stop and finally he purchased a key chain. He told me that this one was better than the others he had. Uncle Leon paid for his purchase and entertained the lady behind the cash register with some idle conversation. It seemed that Uncle Leon was always comfortable talking with women. Of course, he conversed with everyone regardless of sex, but he preferred women more. However, in his defense, Uncle Leon spoke kindly to all women regardless of age or appearance. It also seemed that some women found him rather interesting. He would say a couple of sentences to a woman in an adoring and bashful way and melt her like butter. I pride myself as being a sophisticated conversation piece, but women have to initiate conversations with me or there would be none.

Uncle Leon and I sat at a booth at the eatery of the truck stop. He plucked at his bulbous nose with his fingers and then grabbed a tissue and wheezingly cleared his sinuses. Uncle Leon then commented that the air conditioning in cars and his big rig aggravated his sinuses. Uncle Leon then remarked how his high blood pressure was a constant threat to him being fit to drive a big rig. He mentioned the medications that he was taking to combat high blood pressure. I looked upon Uncle Leon's countenance and saw that the years had been somewhat kind to him but he did look a little tired and weary. The thin age lines etched on his face were due to inadequate sleep and driving million of miles up and down interstate highways.

I knew that driving the highways were wrought with problems for truckers. Truckers have to deal with a variety of weather conditions, and the drivers of smaller vehicles darting in and out of traffic lanes near the big rigs like flies aggravating an elephant. Equally challenging are the uphill and downhill mountainous highways with thousands of pounds of payload either limiting a truck's ascent or expediting the truck's descent.

It seemed that very few things daunted Uncle Leon except on the few occasions that he took his wife, Aunt Shirley, on the road with him. Uncle Leon operated his citizen band radio when Aunt Shirley accompanied him on road trips and other truckers on the same radio frequency as Uncle Leon would have rather explicit conversations. Uncle Leon placed the other drivers on notice that his wife was riding with him and cautioned them to curb their abusive and obscene language. The other big rig drivers grudgingly cleaned up their explicit conversations out of a respect for the Uncle Leon and his wife.

Several other drivers, most of who were wearing baseball caps with trucking and racecar logos on them, were sitting at eating booths near us. The drivers sat with their bodies slightly bent forward and took drags from cigarettes as they conversed with each other in low to medium tones. They were dressed in comfortable cotton pants and blue jeans. Most wore short sleeved, because of the fair weather with the stubble of unshaven hair on their faces. The drivers all appeared relaxed and in no immediate hurry to leave the confines of the diner. This was in stark contrast to their big rigs rolling down the highways and interstates at lightning speeds.

The waitress at the truck stop, an older woman, who was not particularly attractive, walked up to our table. She grinned at Uncle Leon upon recognizing him, called him by name, and asked how he was doing. Uncle Leon greeted the woman and inquired about her health. Uncle Leon had gazed at the menu prior to the waitress arrival and when she asked what he wanted to order, he gazed at the menu for a few seconds and ordered potatoes, meat and gravy. My Uncle then motioned at me to place an order and I ordered just a cup of coffee with cream and sugar. The waitress departed with our orders and my uncle commented that the food at this particular stop was delicious and he stopped here often.

Uncle Leon mentioned that he had acquired a taste for truck stop food and in his opinion, it was the best food a man could eat. I had given the eatery a glancing over since our arrival and saw that it appeared to be a functional eating establishment but the décor did not have any of the extravagances of some of the fancier eateries that I had frequented. The diner reminded me of the mess or chow halls that I frequented during my twenty-year hitch in the army. However, the décor in the army chow halls surpassed that of this truck stop diner.

Within minutes, the waitress returned with Uncle Leon's meal, which was strewn, on a plain white plate. The plate was worn and chipped on the edges. Undoubtedly, this plate had been served in front of thousands of truckers prior to Uncle Leon. The plate bore a healthy portion of white potatoes and meat that were covered generously with thick brown gravy. In my opinion, despite how badly some foods are prepared, a generous covering of delicious gravy is a great way of masking culinary shortcomings. My Uncle then shoved the fork and knife away from him and grasped a tablespoon in his right hand with all fingers and his thumb wrapped around the spoon's handle. Uncle Leon then started shoveling the food into his mouth and chewing at a slow but even pace. He nodded his head and a slight smile creased his face as he savored the taste of his meal. Uncle Leon paused while devouring his food and commented that I was missing a great meal. I could only think that looks are sometimes deceiving, because the meal did not look too appetizing.

However, this eatery was symbolic of a trucker's life on the road. It went hand in hand with the grubby looking motels, bedraggled drivers, and the constant roar of big rigs parked and running in the huge pockmarked parking lot of the truck stop. It was symbolic of men on the go constantly and making scheduled pickups and deliveries at shipping depots. This is not a suit and tie affair with shiny shoes and briefcases.

Driving big rigs is symbolic of cowboys herding long horned steers through the vast territories of our country over one hundred years ago. It is reminiscent of a time when foul weather, extreme conditions and savages were threats to one's livelihood. Despite all the threats, manmade or otherwise, the herd got delivered the majority of the time, which is similar to truckers battling the extremes to get the cargo delivered.

In my opinion, the truckers are modern day heroes or dare devils, who are sometimes forced to use their imagination, wit and strength to get the job done.

Uncle Leon drove a white tractor and trailer and even now, several years after his death, I see many white big rigs travelling on the highways. I often find myself peering at the drivers, though I know it is impossible that Uncle Leon would be driving the trucks. It's just that the big rigs constantly remind me of my uncle and his travels across this vast country of ours. He was dedicated to his profession.

Nowadays, I think that the highways are a lure to a special breed of people. For those people who are looking for excitement and a change of scenery.

However, some people drive for hire to escape some of life's problems. Driving can give a person time and space to relax and reconsider their problems, but then loneliness and other tormented feelings can be a danger to highway driving. I remember an old adage that says that you never know what is down the highway. I guess that is true, but then there can be death and destruction there if personal problems outweigh safety considerations.

I got a lust for the highway or travel myself, because within three years after Uncle Leon's death, I became an independent contractor and performed courier runs on the weekends. I drove about three hundred miles on the weekends to various cities in Northern Virginia near the nation's capitol. Driving for hire was a fulfilling experience and I felt an even closer kinship to my deceased uncle.

I also traveled on the highway, as a courier to reinforce my belief that driving can be a safe adventure if you follow the rules of the road. Then at the same time, I wanted to demonstrate that my uncle is still alive in many ways. Well, he is not here in a physical sense, but he was important in my life. I do homage to his memory by doing the things that he liked.

I try not to be a stranger to the family that he left behind, though I am not with them constantly. I can never take my uncle's place; therefore my visits to his family are consistent to the visits I made while he was alive. I feel that to appreciate the death of a loved one, we should not be shielded by false hopes and dreams. Our deceased loved ones are not going to walk back through the door one day, at least not in this physical world in which we live. As my uncle's nephew, my job is to keep his memory alive. Therefore, he will never be forgotten.

So, we the living, continue to live our lives amidst all of life's triumphs and sorrows until such time that we too will become only memories in the minds of those that we leave behind.

Many people strongly believe that one day we will be reunited for an eternity with those loved ones, who exist now only in our hearts and memories.

Even now, I can envision Uncle Leon with a radiant smile on his face, during our reunion at a future time and place. Perhaps, at the entrance of a trucker's diner.

Chapter Twelve

Pa Daddy's Legacy

(1967-2001)

On December 26, 2000, I arrived at Granny's house in North Carolina for a visit. Four years had past since Uncle Leon's death, but it seemed his tragic accident had happened only a few months earlier. I noticed that most of my grandparents' farm land is now occupied by four modern built houses that are owned by one of Granny's daughters and various grandchildren. Uncle John's house is about one city block up the dirt road from the farm.

Years after Pa Daddy began his self imposed exile from the farm, my relatives began to trickle back there. They built homes on the fertile farmland, where fields of tobacco and corn once flourished.

There are also some of my relatives living on family inherited land in the rural areas of an adjacent county in North Carolina and near our family cemetery. Our relatives, who reside in an adjacent county, live several miles from Granny's farm. In this particular county, there are several houses that are home to Granny's immediate kin. There are also numerous other houses that are owned by Granny's kinfolk, who are descendants of Granny's parents and grandparents.

A few of my relatives still have some negative feelings about Pa Daddy. Perhaps in time, those transcending feelings will fade and they will put the bitterness of the past behind them. However, none can deny that Pa Daddy had some positive influences on their lives. He taught them good work ethics and proper etiquette. However, Pa Daddy was remiss at teaching them how to control their sometime argumentative demeanors.

Some of my relatives still struggle with their emotions about Pa Daddy though he had entered into eternity several years before. Hopefully, someday, like a phoenix they will rise above the despair, put the past behind them, and reorganize their own lives.

Cumulatively, my relatives living at or near the farm have lost husbands, daughters, a mother, wife, sons and a girlfriend over a short period of time to the clutches of death. Death had made its rounds through my family and many tears had fallen. Some of the survivors at the farm suffer with ill health and problems brought on by aging.

Cousin Howard had recently told me that Granny is about one hundred and one years old. Well, a person meeting Granny would never surmise that she is that old. Cousin Howard also has a burning desire to buy a tractor and trailer. He is a man in his early fifties. Uncle Leon was about the same age as Cousin Howard. There was always a strong devotion and trust between them.

Cousin Howard wandered for days after Uncle Leon's death to find answers about the tragedy and to relieve his feelings of frustration and loss.

Howard ventured to the trucking company and viewed the remains of Uncle Leon's demolished truck. Thus he was able to come to grips with the tragedy and obtained a more emotional resolution. Cousin Howard has fond feelings about Uncle Leon though he is gone, and he will always remember him as both an uncle and dear friend.

I parked my pickup truck at the side of Granny's house and noticed that there was a wooden ramp attached to the side of her house to facilitate a wheel chair. I walked inside of the house and spied Uncle John and Granny sitting in the kitchen. Uncle John was sitting on a motorized wheelchair. This was in stark contrast to him crawling up the stairs of Granny's house about four years earlier. Uncle John smiled broadly at me and Granny placed a roaster pan containing a ham and turkey that she had cooked into the oven of her stove. Despite her age, Granny is still cooking and surprisingly she is not senile. Uncle John, who is never at a loss for words, mentioned that he had not seen me since the feud that I had with my older sister, Helen.

It was a feud that developed after my father was slain and about the final disposition of his estate. My father was slain eight months after Uncle Leon's death. It's best to let sleeping dogs lie; therefore I am not going to recount the details of the feud. I can only say that feuds with blood relatives are bitter and should be avoided at all costs.

Uncle John has always been a saber rattler. I was not disappointed when he began to recount Uncle Leon's limited participation around the farm during their younger years. Uncle John continued to harp about Uncle Leon and Granny rolled her eyes up to the ceiling and shook her head. Uncle John then made comments about Pa Daddy by punctuating that neither Pa Daddy nor Uncle Leon told the truth during their lives. Granny then cautioned Uncle John to curb his comments about Uncle Leon and Pa Daddy.

Uncle John then terminated his comments about them but went on another exploit about the repairman who repaired Granny's electrical pump for her well. Uncle John commented that he did not think the repairman was proficient with the repairs and that he sat nearby on his motorized wheel chair to observe him. Uncle John commented that he would have gotten closer to watch the repairs, but the mud would have bogged down his wheelchair. Without a doubt, Uncle John was an irritant to the repairman throughout the repairs. However, Uncle John had the upper hand because a man in a wheelchair is always given more latitude despite his obnoxious behavior. I learned this lesson well while working at the Veterans Affairs Hospital and documenting incidents involving unruly paraplegics and quadriplegics.

Uncle John then made comments about the nine acres of ancestral land that Uncle Leon was care taker of and now is in the hands of Uncle Leon's immediate family. Uncle John then carefully chided Granny for putting Uncle Leon as caretaker when he was at risk driving trucks each day. I softened Uncle John's comments by reminding him that Uncle Leon's two daughters, who are his nieces, my cousins, and Granny grandchildren now control the land. I pointed out that Aunt Shirley ensured that his daughters inherited the land after Uncle Leon's death. I then saw Granny glance at me briefly with a smug expression on her face.

After Uncle John had delivered verbal assaults on relatives both departed and living, Granny began to air Uncle John's dirty laundry. Granny elaborated on how Uncle John was dating a twenty-five year old woman with four children though he is almost seventy years old. I glanced at Uncle John briefly and noticed that he was maintaining his composure. He sat with a poker face throughout Granny's verbal barrage about his social life.

Within a few minutes of my visit, one of my younger aunts, Aunt Virginia, walked into Granny's house, greeted me and sat down. Uncle John then expounded on how Uncle Leon had not told people the truth about his hair. Uncle John explained that Uncle Leon used hair products to relax his hair but lied to people that he had a good grade of hair. I peered at Uncle John and then politely chuckled. I surmised that Uncle John was just rambling on as usual and making conversation, because he would chuckle at his own comments.

Aunt Virginia interrupted Uncle John and then made a strange comment. She remarked that late at night and remarkably after the death of Uncle Leon, she hears the air horn of a tractor and trailer emitting a series of blasts as it passes her house. Aunt Virginia commented that though she hears the horn, she never sees a truck. We all then looked at each other quizzically and Granny then smiled.

Aunt Virginia and Uncle John then got into an in depth discussion about infidelity in marital relationships. Aunt Virginia opinioned that some women needed to wear sexy lingerie, buy new bed sheets and do personal appearance improvement things to keep themselves appealing to their husbands. She stated that it kept some men from straying. Uncle John, who was arrogant as usual, told Aunt Virginia, "Woman, you do not know what you are talking about." Uncle John then threw in his own opinions and punctuated that if people lived according to their wedding vows and the bible, that fancy persuasions would not be needed. Uncle John and Aunt Virginia disagreed with each other comments and raised their voices to argue their positions. Then they started shouting their opinions at each other. Each seeking to gain the upper hand in the conversation.

I shook my head and surmised that nothing had really changed. My family members are growing older physically, but their mentalities remained the same throughout the years. Subconsciously, it seems that Uncle John is still carrying emotional baggage from the past. It seems though he is recounting negative things about his father and brother, that he is doing it with some degree of respect. It is necessary for him to make his peace with his departed father and brother, because he unknowingly may be damaging his own health.

I would be remiss if I did not discuss the issue of guns. I recall being at Uncle Leon's funeral and seeing the telltale bulges in women's pocketbooks and men's pockets. It seemed that the past tragedy at the farm would have discouraged my family members from carrying guns. However, some people forget about the ramifications of past tragedies too soon.

Needless to say, guns are instruments of death and destruction. When people bring guns into fights to gain the upper hand, they either achieve their goals or things get reversed and they end up being killed by their own guns. Some people brandish guns to instill fear in other people and to show that they are serious or mean business. The adage that an empty gun is a loaded gun is very true. Just when a person assumes that he or she unloaded the gun the last time that they used it, the gun fires a bullet and someone is struck. Sometimes the person, who pulled the trigger while playfully scaring a friend or relative, is shocked that the gun fired and pulls the trigger again. Then their friend or relative is the recipient of two bullets. The person firing the gun is further shocked when he or she hear the words, "You have the right to remain silent." Those words are a preamble to hard times in someone's immediate future.

I read in a local newspaper that it costs $20,000 to remove a bullet from a person and there are no discounts given for removing additional bullets. Therefore, removing two bullets from a person would cost $40,000. I feel that I am in the wrong occupation. Physicians and undertakers are profitable occupations, given all of the needless violence that occurs in our society. I saw a television special, where an undertaker was making so much money from gang violence, that he gave one gang member a free funeral. I am not trying to be morbid, but I can find better things to do with my time than shoot people.

Equally interesting, are the excuses from people who shot other people. "Well, officer, he jumped as I pulled the trigger and I struck an innocent bystander." I guess intended victims are supposed to stand still while being shot at and wear a bull's eye as wide as a barn. I say this because some people can not shoot what they are pointing at, therefore there is a loose bullet flying around and it has no friends.

Nowadays, when terrible tragedies occur, counseling is provided to those people who were affected by the tragedies. In this way, they are better able to cope with the tragedies and live more productive lives.

Burying tragedies as secrets is not a healthy way of dealing with them. The adage about burying the dead and going on with life is very true. People must allow themselves to mourn and feel

115

all of the emotions that come with losing a loved one. Stifling those emotions will only have negative consequences in the lives of those who try to deny their feelings for loved ones. When I look in the mirror, I see not only myself, but my father, mother, and other ancestors, who lived before me. They are I and I am them. I would be foolish to deny my feelings for them despite what might happen. The consequences of denying feelings for loved ones are not promising.

Overall, my family members are great people. They are very kindhearted and considerate. However, there is the issue of respect and it has always been critical to any family's orderly coexistence. Also, petty jealousies can be stumbling blocks in how family members react to each other.

One thing is for certain. We come into this world with nothing, and we will depart this life with nothing. Death is afforded to all of us equally, though there are various ways of coming to one's life end.

My Uncle Leon was successful during his life, because he was willing to make certain sacrifices. He was not perfect and no one else is either. Uncle Leon was only one man, and he had certain commitments to his immediate family or his wife and children. His family continues to reap from his success. His immediate family is my relatives; therefore they have my everlasting support.

Situations occurred at our family farm and one of them was a tragic accident. The accident, without doubt, initiated a chain of events that would change some of my relatives' lives. Things could have been different with the lives of some of my family members today if not for that tragic accident. The accident caused bitterness and discouragement, but in the end it did propel some people to strike out on their own and build themselves successful lives. This is the way that life works, because the events of life bring both triumphs and sorrows.

I carried a heavier burden than other relatives because of the tragic accident. Both of my parents were deeply affected by it. The pitfalls of the tragedy caused me to try harder, thus I succeeded.

My father was torn between many emotions by the tragedy but he remained strong in his beliefs. Four months before my father's untimely death, we met and I saw before me an old man who had survived life's struggles. He had seen death up close and in a personal way. On that day, my father and I put the past behind us and symbolically forgave each other for the negative interactions we had during the past. I was thankful for that opportunity. We had both learned that you can not hold innocent people accountable for the wrongful acts of others. We must review what happened and consider the rationale and reasons for it happening.

On that particular day, I noticed for the first time how old and gray my father was. I mentioned to my father that he had never discussed his burial plans with us, his children. Though my father was about seventy-five years old, he seemed shocked that I had initiated such a conversation. My father paused and then his face softened. He then told me that he wanted to be buried beside his mother and uncle. My father explained that his mother and uncle were buried a few miles from the house that he inherited from his mother. I then asked my father to show me where his mother and uncle were buried, as I had never visited their graves. It was during the early summer of 1997 when my father and I had our conversation. We decided that we would meet during October or November of 1997 and go together to visit the gravesites.

Also on that particular day, I took my father shopping and purchased him some of his favorite foods and beverages. My father was very happy that day.

Several months later during October 1997, he succumbed from a head wound that he sustained during a petty argument with a friend.

My sister, Helen, and I went to the adjacent county prior to my father's funeral to locate his mother's gravesite. We spoke with a woman first cousin of our father in the rural area of the county where my father and his mother once lived. The woman was older than my sister and me. She made some pleasant remarks about my father and his mother. The woman also recounted the story about my paternal grandmother being the first person to arrive at her uncle's house after his death. The woman joked that the uncle's safe had less cash when other family member's arrived.

The woman instructed us how to find my grandmother's grave, but she advised us that the gravesite was situated behind someone's house. My father's cousin also stated that the gravesites might be inaccessible because of brush and small trees.

My sister and I drove to the approximate location of where the gravesite is located, but noticed that the area was thick with brush and trees. The gravesite was inaccessible; therefore we were not able to bury my father beside his mother. The funeral was two days away and it would have required heavy equipment to clear the area for a proper burial.

My sister and I then elected to bury my father in perpetual care cemetery that is located several blocks from the neighborhood where we lived as children. This is my father's current resting place, but I have not forgotten his request that he made several months before his death.

Another problem that my sister and I encountered concerning our paternal grandmother's gravesite location, is the fact that her grave is on the land of a distant relative of ours. It would have been imposing to ask for permission to bury yet another person behind his house. However, the possibility of my father and his mother resting beside each other is not impossible. I recall an old adage about taking someone or something to the mountain instead of bringing the mountain to them. I can not recall the adage completely right now, but I think that the point has been made. Granted, I am getting older and working with a slight memory handicap.

My father's death was ruled as manslaughter and the offender was incarcerated for a few years. I consulted with the prosecutor and agreed that the incident should not be tried in court. The offender agreed to a plea bargain arrangement. Since I was educated in the field of criminal justice and aware of all of the particulars concerning the incident, I was satisfied with the plea bargain arrangement. Some of my immediate family members had visions of the offender toiling at hard labor and in prison for scores of years, but the crime did not call for such a harsh punishment. In the scheme of things, my father lived to be about seventy-five years old, which is remarkable nowadays, given all the crimes of violence that occur.

Foremost, there must be the willingness to forgive. I have forgiven the person who caused my father's death. There was no need for me to forgive my grandfather, because he openly admitted his error. The integrity of his character supported that the tragedy was an accident.

I have expressed forgiveness strongly within my heart and hold no malice towards anyone. Therefore, in the future, when my appointed time comes, I can depart this world without the burdens of bitterness and hate in my heart. So, if you are bitter and bear hate, I encourage you to lift and rid yourself of those burdens. Perhaps you do not believe in fate and destiny, but one thing is for certain, you are going to be called home one day. However, you do not know when you will be summoned.

Conscience: *This sure was a wild story that you pieced together. A story of death, the supernatural, love, compassion, caring, forgiveness, destiny, and fate. I don't know if people are going to believe that your story is a true one. Well, all of the events you portrayed did occur.*

Yes, unfortunately, all that is written here did occur. However, I have always felt that one pays a price, when he goes back into the past and recalls painful events. There were both good times and bad times, but by writing about them, in a sense, I have re-lived those events. I felt all of the emotions, joy, anguish, sorrow and pain from the past.

Reliving the past has shown me that there are some things that I must do. I will insure that my relatives, who lie in hallowed grounds, are appropriately honored. This is what we the living must always do, because people who fail to honor their dead are without honor themselves.

It seemed that I had a dream the other night. My family finally had a reunion and Granny our matriarch is there. The reunion seemed fitting because Granny is nearly a hundred years old; there-fore she has the right to see all of her children, grandchildren, great grandchildren and great-great grandchildren at a reunion. Undoubtedly, Granny has earned the right to a reunion. The re-union would represent five generations of family members. It's rare to have that many generations of a family at a reunion. I need to go to such a reunion because there are relatives that I have never met.

In the dream, it seemed that my family's spiritual ancestors from past lives assembled and looked on joyously at the reunion. Even the goddesses of fate paused in their weaving and commented, "Well, it's a step in the right direction. We will be cutting less threads than usual for that family now." *"Sign posted: All persons entering this reunion will check their firearms, bludgeons, and other items that can inflict bodily harm at the door."*

EPILOGUE

I realize or know now that my uncle made some miscalculations while driving. Uncle Leon let the truck drive him instead of him driving it. I am not making any judgments, because I have made some mistakes during my life also. It's just that my mistakes were salvageable, thus I was spared.

I reflect back on the numerous fatal automobile accidents I have investigated. The accidents were either alcohol related, speed excessive for weather, traffic and road conditions or people modifying cars and driving them at speeds well beyond the manufacturer's expectations. It was either the aforementioned things that killed people or people having what they think is a lot of courage. I call it tombstone courage, because that kind of courage will earn you a tombstone over your body at the graveyard. The human race can build and manufacture great things, but we sure can not repair and bring back the dead.

Uncle Leon did not die in vain, because his death has caused me to reevaluate my own life. Undoubtedly, Uncle Leon was a shining star to our family during times of our darkest despairs. It was an honor and privilege for me to have known him. I will surely miss him.

I can only say now that if there is a need for a trucker somewhere in the after life, that my Uncle Leon is the spirit for the job. Uncle Leon hauled lots of freight and drove more miles on the highway than any other driver at the trucking firm.

During all of my visits to Uncle Leon's grave, I always look back at his grave before departing. I always honor him by saying, "Keep on trucking good buddy."

Uncle Leon's mother, who is about one hundred years old, will tell you that Uncle Leon is not dead. Granny will tell you that Leon was always on the road during life and that is where he is at now. On the road.

THE END

IN REMEMBRANCE OF GRANNY

GRANNY

March 20, 1900- February 27,2001

Granny entered into eternity a few weeks prior to the first publishing of this book. I was able to speak with her a few days before her death while she was in the hospital. I mentioned some scenes in this book and described how she was characterized. Granny laughed and was happy. I told Granny that she was at the top of the guest list for a family reunion this year .There were indications at that time that Granny would stay at the hospital for about two more days and return home on the weekend. However, on February 24, 2001, Granny's health rapidly declined while still at the hospital.

I arrived at the hospital on February 26, 2001 and visited with Granny. The prognosis was grim. It seemed that it would take a miracle to bring Granny back to good health. Uncle Stephanie commented that the miracle had already happened, given Granny's longevity. I agreed with his statement. I knew in my heart that the end was near, and I was at the hospital during the final hours before Granny's death.

During the wee hours of February 27, 2001, Granny entered into eternity. Cousin Andrea, who is a registered nurse, attended to her. Several other family members and I arrived at the hospital after being summoned by Cousin Andrea about Granny's impending death.

Earlier, Uncle John told me at the hospital that he wanted God to take him instead of Granny. I assumed that some other relatives might have had similar thoughts. However, this was Granny's home going and God had decided to call his humble servant home.

Granny had lived over one hundred years and was an invaluable asset to her family. A few years prior to her death, Granny deeded out tracts of her farmland to her children and grandchildren as she had promised. Granny was a wise woman and did this to preclude any controversies after her death. However, prior to her death, certain relatives gave Granny untruthful information to sway her opinions about the division of her estate. At one point, I sent a letter to Granny and several of my family members to correct some statements that certain family member(s) had made to Granny. The sin of untruthfulness or lying has caused death and other calamities throughout history. I had the utmost respect for Granny and never lied to her or wrongfully influenced her to make opinions about other family members.

There is a term called reconciliation. For me, this means evaluating what has occurred and coming to a correct conclusion. This term is going to be important, when people stand in front of their creator, who will make conclusions about how they lived their lives. But since the creator knows all, lies and untruths on the day of judgement will be conclusive in a negative way.

Therefore, I invite people of questionable character to do self-evaluations, and make some corrections.

Granny's funeral was similar to that of a page from a storybook with many pink and white floral wreaths. We viewed Granny's remains and it seemed that she was a woman aged fifty and not one hundred. Clean living and consistent work ethic preserved granny.

Cousin Andrea, Cousin Peter and I eulogized Granny at her funeral. I had enclosed an insert in Granny's funeral program that she is a character in this book. Aunt Della's sister-in-law, Dorothy, asked me during the funeral services to read the contents of the insert in church. I had not prepared a eulogy speech for Granny, because I did not intend to speak. However, after Cousin Andrea had attempted to deliver her eulogy and was overcome with grief, I decided that I would do more than read just the contents of the insert.

When I stepped up into the pulpit, suddenly I had a feeling of elation. With my voice booming and echoing throughout the church, I mentioned that Granny is a character in this book. I stated that Granny exemplified honesty, integrity and free heartiness and that people around the world would read this book and know about Granny's character. I reminded the mourners that death is an inevitable consequence of being born.

I then pointed out that though Granny had departed her earthly bounds, she had gone to a better place. I told the mourners that Granny would challenge them to come to where she is at now. I stated that Granny would also say that some of the mourners must change their ways to get to where she is. I then recounted a story about Granny having five watermelons and that she told visiting relatives to take the biggest of the watermelons until all of the watermelons were gone. I pointed out the Granny was not selfish and gave freely to other people. However, I did not mention in the story to the mourners that the watermelons belonged to me and that I had left them with Granny for safekeeping. I was shocked when I returned from work and saw that three watermelons were gone. I asked Granny about the situation and with a stern expression on her face, she taught me about sharing. Granny's lesson was valuable. I realized that other people have needs and realistically I could not have consumed five watermelons. Some of the watermelons would have rotted before I could have consumed them. There are also consequences from the sin of gluttony, and they are obvious when some people look in the mirror.

Cousin Peter then eulogized Granny after my speech and spoke of Granny's good deeds. Cousin Peter also stated that people entering into eternity is a joyous occasion and that we should not fear death.

Granny was always there with a helping hand. Granny

never broke a promise and she never lied to people in her family. She bailed family culprits out of jail, gave money to help those with personal endeavors, and soothed the mental and physical wounds of her family. She helped with the care of her grandchildren, great grandchildren, and great-great grandchildren. Granny never asked relatives when would they return to retrieve their children. She just cared for them until the parents returned.

Though Granny was never in the military service, she saw action during many family feuds and arguments. From the World War II Era to the War in Bosnia, Granny symbolically wore helmets and flak vests and carried white flags while mediating peace between family members. On occasions, Granny had to do some physical grappling, brandish walking canes and use other means to cool some situations.

Granny carried out her peace- keeping duties up to the time that she entered into eternity. She also cooked for younger family members that were either ill or just did not want to cook. Of course, Granny had many good times and would chuckle in remembrance of some of the situations that she rectified. As I had always envisioned, Granny was working and active up to the end.

Many people talk about heaven. I think that heaven after we depart our earthly bounds, is what we like the most. Even now, I can envision Granny in a better place, wearing a wide brim straw hat on her head and looking with awe at flourishing fields and livestock. I can imagine her on a farm that is a replica of her place in the country. However, it is a farm without sorrow, pain, sickness or toil. Even I would call that heaven.

I hope that Granny holds a bunk open for me at her farm, because one of these days in the future, I will be making a visit there myself. However, I will bide my time and walk down that path when destiny beckons me.

Soon, I will return to North Carolina, visit Granny's gravesite and reminisce about her good deeds. I will also visit Pa Daddy's grave, which is beside Granny's grave and my father's grave, which is in proximity of my grandparents' graves. I will pay my respects to them and then travel to a nearby county to see my Aunt Della.

My Aunt Della has promised to provide me with information concerning our family history. She will recount information and details about our ancestors from the time of the Emancipation Proclamation to present. I will document her stories, do some research and write sequels to "The Winds of Destiny". Therefore in the near future, use Internet search engines and input "The Winds of Destiny" or "Willie Tee" and you will be able to view either my ongoing projects or leave feedback about this book.

On the next page is an insert that I created for Granny's funeral program and it was available for the mourners at her funeral.

I would like to extend my warmest thanks to the Adkins-Drain Funeral Home of Wilmington, North Carolina, for their thorough and professional services. Their professionalism helped my family daring their time of sorrow.

FOR

My Grandmother

(Granny)

(The excerpt below is from the nonfiction book: The Winds of Destiny)

I was always happy to see Granny in town shopping. She always had a few spare coins to give me. Granny would always recount some bad event that had occurred according to the news. She would shake her head and comment that it was just terrible. Granny would use words like "dirty dogs" to describe the persons who had committed certain crimes. She would always close her comments by stating, "What is this world coming to?"

In my opinion, Granny has always thrived to live her life according to strict morals and rules. I have never seen her smoke or consume alcoholic beverages. Undoubtedly, Granny expects other people to be law abiding and decent in their interactions with others. I think that this is the reason why Granny has preferred to live in the rural areas or country all of her life. Rural living is away from the congested cities and it seems that country folk are more endearing and have more respect for their fellow man.

I yearn even now for the sweet smell of blossom trees,
    that line the fields in the country.
I yearn to look upon fertile fields where crops flourish
    and smell the sweet essences of nature.

To see flocks of birds fluttering overhead against a clear blue sky,
    and hear the sounds of birds chirping and singing in trees.

I want to drink crisp and sweet water from a well and strode down
    dusty roads and paths where my ancestors once walked.

Once a person has experienced all of these things,
    one day he or she will be encouraged,
To return home to the country.

God's speed Granny on your voyage into eternity.

    With Everlasting Love and Devotion,

FROM: Willie Tee, your grandson, the Author
      of: "The Winds of Destiny"

BLIBIOGRAPHY

"Fates" Microsoft ® Encarta ® Online Encyclopedia 2000
http://encarta.msn.com © 1997-2000 Microsoft Corporation.
All rights reserved.

ABOUT THE AUTHOR

NAME: Willie Tee (pen name)

PERSONAL INFORMATION: Willie was born June 21, 1955 at North Carolina. He attended school, elementary through high school, at Wilmington, North Carolina.

FAMILY: Willie has a wife, Ruth, a daughter April, and a son Frederick, who are adults. Willie resides with his wife and granddaughter, Janina at Chesterfield County, Virginia. Willie has another granddaughter, Lisa Marie, who resides near Bamberg, Germany.

HOBBIES: Willie enjoys travel, fishing, reading, writing essays and poems and chatting on the Internet.

MEMBERSHIPS: Retired U.S. Army Staff Sergeant; The American Legion, Alpha Phi Sigma, Omega Mu Chapter (National Criminal Justice Honor Society); Alumni, Virginia Commonwealth University, Richmond, Virginia; Alumni, John Tyler Community College, Chesterfield Virginia.

EDUCATION: Bachelors of Science Degree, Criminal Justice; Associate Applied Science Degree, Police Science, (Magna Cum Laude).

CURRENT OCCUPATION: Consumer Affairs Investigator, Office of Consumer Affairs.

SYNOPSIS: Willie Tee was born at North Carolina and lived in the rural areas at family farms until he was six years old. Willie's book portrays some scenes of farm life during the late 1950s. Willie moved to Wilmington, North Carolina with his parents during 1961 and resided there until he enlisted in the United States Army Military Police Corps during 1974. Willie wrote a short story titled, "Death Takes a Holiday" for his Junior High School newspaper. It was a mystery story like "The Winds of Destiny" is.

Willie wrote thousands of investigative reports while employed as an investigator and police officer. His vast writing experience in the criminal justice field are apparent from his well organized and explicit literary documents.

Willie investigates consumer complaints and teaches consumer awareness to the public.

Book Purchasing Information

This book (Second Edition) can be purchased at most major book stores or on the Internet at Amazon.com. This book was traditionally published to be available on bookstores shelves. However, the original version of The Winds of Destiny, is a print on demand book that can be ordered through Barnes & Noble, Books A Million, Chapter Eleven Bookstores, and most independent bookstores. Print on demand books are best purchased at the publisher's Internet site, www.1stbooks.com/bookview/6354 or major bookstores' Internet Sites. Some readers telephone local bookstores and order the print on demand version, which is delivered within a short time to the bookstores. Please note that there are few differences in context between the original edition and second edition of this book. Persons who are not avid readers will find the second edition easier to navigate.

Visit Willie on the Internet at www.authorsden.com/willietee and be eligible to win $200.00 cash prizes and free books. You can also leave messages at Willie's web site about his book. The following are major events that Willie will attend this year:

Virginia Festival of the Book, Charlottesville, VA, 20 March 2002
North Carolina Azalea Festival, Wilmington, N.C. 6 April 2002
Memphis Black Writer's Conference, Memphis, TN 18-20 April 2002
Southern Festival of Books, Nashville, TN, 11-13 October 2002

Book Distributors, fundraisers, foundations, and independent bookstore owners can purchase *The Winds of Destiny, Second Edition*, wholesale through R&B Trading Company, telephone 804-739-8073, Fax: 775-243-6578, email: Dwindsofdestiny@aol.com.

Unsold wholesale copies of the book (*Second Edition*) can be returned to R&B for a refund. The original version of the book (print on demand) is still being sold by 1st Books Library and wholesale at www.1stbooks.com/bookview/6354 or telephone book ordering specialist at 1-888-280-7715. The wholesale return policy on print on demand books is subject to change in the near future.

Readers residing at Richmond, Virginia can purchase this book at the One Force Bookstore, 217 East Clay Street, Richmond, Virginia

I know that you enjoyed reading my book and hope that you will buy the sequels of *The Winds of Destiny* during the future. My family and I extend our thanks to the readers and other business associates. May God continue to shower his blessings upon you.

Many Thanks,

Willie Tee